D0423369

PRESENTED TO

FROM

ON THE OCCASION OF

LIFE PROMISES™
FOR LEADERS

inspirational Scriptures and devotional thoughts

ZIG ZIGLAR

Tyndale House Publishers, Inc. · Carol Stream, Illinois

Visit Tyndale online at www.tyndale.com.

TYNDALE and Tyndale's quill logo are registered trademarks of Tyndale House Publishers, Inc.

Life Promises is a trademark of Tyndale House Publishers, Inc.

Designed by Ron Kaufmann

Published in association with Yates & Yates (www.yates2.com).

Library of Congress Cataloging-in-Publication Data

Ziglar, Zig.
  Life promises for leaders : inspirational Scriptures and devotional thoughts / Zig Ziglar.
      p. cm. — (Life promises)
  Includes index.
  ISBN 978-1-4143-6462-9 (hc)
1. Leadership—Biblical teaching. I. Title.
  BS680.L4Z54 2012
  242'.68—dc23   2012011651

Printed in China

18 17 16 15 14 13 12
 7   6   5   4   3   2   1

LIFE PROMISES

I [Paul] do not count myself to have apprehended; but one thing I do, forgetting those things which are behind and reaching forward to those things which are ahead, I press toward the goal for the prize of the upward call of God in Christ Jesus.
PHILIPPIANS 3:13-14

Faith is the substance of things hoped for, the evidence of things not seen.
HEBREWS 11:1

God has not given us a spirit of fear, but of power and of love and of a sound mind.
2 TIMOTHY 1:7

ONE THING

PAUL WAS THE GREATEST LEADER in the history of the church, but he wasn't cocky. He knew he was still a work in progress. His days were filled with starting churches, managing leaders, and taking the gospel to everyone in the known world, but he reduced his job description to "one thing," or in management terms, *the rigorous commitment to a singular objective* that has two parts: not dwelling on the past, but reaching ahead to achieve the vision of the future.

The past can bog us down in different ways: Some of us feel ashamed by failures in our personal lives or in business, and every decision we make is colored by the fear that we'll make the same mistake again. Others of us live in past glories. We've enjoyed stunning success, but instead of using our gains as a foundation for future growth, we keep reliving those memories. Living in the past, whether failed or successful, takes our lives out of focus.

Paul says, "Forget the past and move on," and he encourages us to uncover and embrace a God-sized cause, one that has a positive impact on people and expands His Kingdom.

What are some past failures or successes you need to leave behind?

Is there a God-sized cause that has gripped your heart?

LIFE PROMISES

The LORD answered . . . and said:

"Write the vision
    And make it plain on tablets,
    That he may run who reads it.
        For the vision is yet for an
            appointed time;
    But at the end it will speak, and it
        will not lie.
    Though it tarries, wait for it."
HABAKKUK 2:2-3

Let us hold fast the confession of our
hope without wavering, for He who
promised is faithful.
HEBREWS 10:23

Let us run with endurance the race that
is set before us, looking unto Jesus, the
author and finisher of our faith, who for
the joy that was set before Him endured
the cross, despising the shame, and has
sat down at the right hand of the throne
of God.
HEBREWS 12:1-2

WRITE IT DOWN!

SOME OF US WANDER from one thing to another our whole lives. We're capable of so much more, but we have never clarified our purpose in life. An out-of-focus purpose can't inspire us, but a crystal-clear lens on God's purpose for us rivets our attention and gives us energy to keep going until we reach our goals.

While the prophet Habakkuk was in prayer, God told him to write down the vision He was giving him. We need to write our vision down in clear, compelling language so that it grips our hearts. A clearly written vision statement frees us from confusion so that we can "run" instead of wander, stumble, or go backward. A clear vision overcomes inertia and produces the inspiration to run toward our goals.

But the fulfillment of our vision is in His timing, not ours. Seldom does anyone move in a straight line from the conception of a dream to its fulfillment. Far more often, we experience ups and downs, delays and disappointments. These, though, won't stop us if we keep our eyes on our purpose and on the One who has given it to us.

Do you have a clear, compelling vision statement?

What would it (or does it) mean to you to have one?

LIFE PROMISES

Whatever your hand finds to do, do it with your might.

ECCLESIASTES 9:10

As each one has received a gift, minister it to one another, as good stewards of the manifold grace of God. . . . If anyone ministers, let him do it as with the ability which God supplies, that in all things God may be glorified through Jesus Christ.

1 PETER 4:10-11

Work with enthusiasm, as though you were working for the Lord rather than for people. Remember that the Lord will reward each one of us for the good we do.

EPHESIANS 6:7-8, NLT

DO YOUR VERY BEST

SOMETIMES, GOD'S DESIRE FOR US is to do our very best even though we don't quite fit the job. When Nehemiah went back to Jerusalem to rebuild the walls of the city, the place was in terrible shape. His job looked hopeless, but Nehemiah believed God could do the impossible. He rallied the people and put them to work carrying stones, framing doors, and defending one another from attacks.

In Nehemiah's story, we find people pitching in where they were needed. Uzziel was a master gold-smith, but when he was asked to carry huge rocks, he never complained. He just worked. And next to him, Hananiah carried stones too. This guy's regular work was making perfume, not slinging mortar, swinging a hammer, or lugging rocks! But he worked hard next to the goldsmith.

Perhaps those around you complain when their work doesn't perfectly match their skills. Don't let their attitude poison you. Instead, roll up your sleeves and do whatever it takes to get the job done. You'll win the trust of your boss and the respect of your peers—and you might even enjoy it!

What are you tempted to complain about at work?

How long should you do a job that doesn't fit you?

See Nehemiah 3.

The wicked flee when no one pursues,
    But the righteous are bold as a lion.
PROVERBS 28:1

If your gift is to encourage others, be
encouraging. If it is giving, give generously. If God has given you leadership
ability, take the responsibility seriously.
And if you have a gift for showing
kindness to others, do it gladly.
ROMANS 12:8, NLT

I know . . . , my God, that You test the
heart and have pleasure in uprightness.
As for me, in the uprightness of my
heart I have willingly offered all these
things; and now with joy I have seen
Your people, who are present here to
offer willingly to You.
1 CHRONICLES 29:17

INTEGRITY

WE KNOW KING DAVID as one of the most gifted leaders the world has ever known. His bravery inspired incredible exploits by the Mighty Men, his battle strategy won many conflicts, and he welded the divided kingdom back together with his diplomatic skill. If we look back to his younger years, we find that his leadership skills and character were shaped during years of obscurity on the hillsides tending sheep.

During those seemingly empty years, day after day and night after night, he paid attention to the task before him. He led the sheep to better pastures and fresh water, and he killed a lion and a bear that attacked them. Alone with his thoughts, he prayed, reflected, and developed literary skill as he wrote his prayers to God. When the time came for David to act to rescue Israel from Goliath and the Philistines, his heart was strong and his hands had been trained.

Some of us find ourselves living and serving in obscurity. David's example helps us to stay in the game, to sharpen our skills, and to strengthen our hearts so we're ready when the time comes to act.

Describe times in your life when you felt passed by. How did you respond?

What are some things you can do to sharpen your skills and strengthen your heart?

See Psalm 78:70-72.

LIFE PROMISES

The word of the LORD is right,
  And all His work is done in truth.
PSALM 33:4

Let nothing be done through selfish
ambition or conceit, but in lowliness
of mind let each esteem others better
than himself.
PHILIPPIANS 2:3

The plans of the diligent lead surely
      to plenty,
    But those of everyone who is hasty,
      surely to poverty.
PROVERBS 21:5

GETTING BACK TO WORK

IF THE MEASURE OF A MAN is how much it takes to get him to quit, then Nehemiah would rank near the top of anyone's list. He began with the almost impossible task of rebuilding the walls of Jerusalem, but he and his builders soon encountered betrayal from their own ranks and opposition from outside.

At one point, some locals insulted the builders to discourage them. When that didn't work and the building continued, their enemies plotted to attack Nehemiah's builders. The people got wind of the impending danger, and they came close to panic. Nehemiah, though, coolly and calmly gave orders to deploy the people so that they felt responsible for those near them.

Nehemiah's leadership saved the day. He knew that the best thing for his builders was for them to get back to work. They wouldn't be safe until the walls were rebuilt, and they couldn't afford to waste time. As leaders, our first instinct shouldn't be to take a break after a success. Sometimes it's appropriate; but often, we need to get back to work so we can capitalize on our success.

When is taking a break a good thing to do?

When is it best to get back to work immediately?

See Nehemiah 4.

LIFE PROMISES

The earth is the Lord's, and all its
      fullness,
    The world and those who dwell
      therein.
PSALM 24:1

As iron sharpens iron,
    So a man sharpens the countenance
      of his friend.
PROVERBS 27:17

The generous soul will be made rich,
    And he who waters will also be
      watered himself.
PROVERBS 11:25

OWNER OR MANAGER

IN A CAPITALIST ECONOMY, ownership is a cornerstone of society. We earn money and buy things, and we consider those things to be ours. But the Bible has a different twist on capitalism. The earth and everything in it were created by God, and as the Creator, He is the rightful owner. He entrusts parts to us for a short time, but we're wise to see ourselves as managers instead of owners.

A consumer mentality values things and people for what they do for us. If they make us feel happy, we like them; if they don't make us feel good, we get rid of them. But as God-appointed managers, we acknowledge that everything—money, family, friendships, neighbors, and coworkers—belongs to the Lord. With that knowledge, we may change some of our spending habits, and we might devote more of our time, energy, and resources to the things that matter most to God.

People are what matter most to Him. He has put us in relationships with others for a purpose, and we need to relate to these people in a way that encourages them and honors Him.

How would it affect your management of money and other resources if you saw yourself as God's appointed manager?

How would it affect your relationships if you saw people as entrusted to you by God?

LIFE PROMISES

Cast away from you all the transgressions which you have committed, and get yourselves a new heart and a new spirit.
EZEKIEL 18:31

Whoever desires to become great among you, let him be your servant.
MATTHEW 20:26

As the LORD lives, whatever the LORD says to me, that I will speak.
1 KINGS 22:14

THE PARADOX OF LEADERSHIP

IN HIS OUTSTANDING BOOK *Good to Great*, Jim Collins describes a mistake many companies make when they hire a CEO. Too often, they try to get a charismatic leader who demands to be the center of attention and receive all the praise. In stark contrast, Collins observed that the most successful companies have leaders who lead with passion, but they are happy to give plenty of credit to anyone and everyone else.[1]

Collins's observations fit perfectly with Jesus' leadership strategy. Jesus told His followers to show their greatness by serving. He then dispelled any misconceptions of what it means to be a servant by picking up a towel and washing the dirty feet of the men at the table with Him.

What does it mean for us to be servants of those in our families and at work? If we follow Jesus' example, we take time to do the most humble tasks: washing dishes, cleaning, sweeping, or even helping an intern with a task.

What impact do "center-of-attention leaders" have on those under them? What impact do "passionate leaders" have on people?

What are two things you can do today to be a servant to those around you?

See John 13:3-14.

---

1 Jim Collins, *Good to Great: Why Some Companies Make the Leap . . . and Others Don't* (New York: HarperCollins, 2001).

LIFE PROMISES

This is the day the Lord has made;
    We will rejoice and be glad in it.
PSALM 118:24

Be still, and know that I am God.
PSALM 46:10

The Lord your God, who goes before
you, He will fight for you.
DEUTERONOMY 1:30

START EACH DAY RIGHT

DEAD-END JOBS, strained relationships, feelings of emptiness—too often, we dread getting up in the morning to face another day of struggles and disappointments. But it doesn't have to be this way. Perspective makes all the difference, and if we have a strong sense of hope in a God of infinite possibilities, the whole world opens up to us.

Imagine Jesus' disciples getting up each morning. Do you think they dreaded the day? Not a chance! Every day was amazing! They watched Jesus heal the sick, raise the dead, cure lepers, argue with the rigid religious leaders, laugh, cry, teach thousands, calm storms, cast out demons, pray all night, and get away to relax.

He's with *us*, too. We don't walk on dusty roads in Palestine, but Christ is with us in the boardroom, the bathroom, and the bedroom. He has made each day for each of us to experience His presence and His power. The disciples often didn't understand what He was doing, and there will be times we don't get it, either. But every day is a gift from God for us to watch Him work in us, around us, and through us.

What would it have been like to be one of the disciples and watch Jesus every day?

How does it affect your attitude about today to realize that you walk with the risen Christ and that today is His gift to you?

LIFE PROMISES

[Jesus said,] "Take My yoke upon you and learn from Me, for I am gentle and lowly in heart, and you will find rest for your souls. For My yoke is easy and My burden is light."

MATTHEW 11:29-30

Create in me a clean heart, O God,
  And renew a steadfast spirit
    within me.

PSALM 51:10

He makes me to lie down in green
    pastures;
  He leads me beside the still waters.
He restores my soul.

PSALM 23:2-3

REST FOR THE SOUL

SOME OF US ARE SO BURDENED by life's pressures that our concept of rest is complete escape from all responsibilities. Although that's not a bad idea, passivity and escape aren't what Jesus had in mind when He was speaking to His followers.

Jesus, in Matthew 11, paints a word picture of a pair of oxen pulling a wagon. Typically, a pair consists of a mature, experienced ox and a young one just learning how to work. The mature ox does far more of the actual work to pull the load. The young animal's task is to figure out how to walk in tandem with the older ox so that they don't pull against each other.

In the same way, Christ invites us to learn to pull alongside Him. When we have difficulties figuring out how to pull our weight and how to walk along with Him, He doesn't scold us. He's gentle and humble, patiently reminding us of who's pulling most of the load. When we learn this lesson, we receive peace, relief, rest, and a heart full of thankfulness for God's leading and strength.

How are you doing in the yoke as you learn to pull with Jesus?

What changes do you need to make? How will these affect your life?

LIFE PROMISES

God resists the proud,
But gives grace to the humble.
JAMES 4:6

The sacrifices of God are a broken spirit,
A broken and a contrite heart—
These, O God, You will not despise.
PSALM 51:17

God forbid that I should boast except in
the cross of our Lord Jesus Christ.
GALATIANS 6:14

RUNNING WILD

HUMILITY CAN BE A DIFFICULT CONCEPT for us to grasp. It is often thought of as being weak or spineless, but that is the wrong definition. A fitting example of humility can be found in the responsiveness of a fine horse to its rider's gentle tug on the reins. When the horse was acquired, it may have been a wild bronco, but it has been broken and now gladly responds to its master's care and guidance.

In His kindness, God allows difficulties into our lives to break us, not to harm us but to tame the selfishness in our hearts. As long as we buck, we fight against God and His gracious purposes for us, but when we finally give in and accept His leadership in our lives, we experience more encouragement, strength, freedom, and joy than we ever imagined.

The "freedom" of the proud is an illusion. Rebellion ultimately results in shattered dreams and shattered lives. But when we are open to God's discipline and leading, we have the chance to experience the true riches of His grace.

What are some ways you've seen God resist the proud?

Would you say you have been broken, you are being broken, or you are still running wild?

LIFE PROMISES

No one can serve two masters; for either he will hate the one and love the other, or else he will be loyal to the one and despise the other. You cannot serve God and mammon.

MATTHEW 6:24

Be . . . fervent in spirit, serving the Lord; rejoicing in hope, patient in tribulation, continuing steadfastly in prayer.

ROMANS 12:10-12

God blesses those who patiently endure testing and temptation. Afterward they will receive the crown of life that God has promised to those who love him.

JAMES 1:12, NLT

WHAT'S IN YOUR BOX?

AT THE STORE, a father gave his son an empty box and said, "Son, you can have anything you want, but you can have only *one* thing. Make a good choice." In a sense, God gives each of us the same opportunity. A million things compete for our affections and our attention, but only one can be on the throne of our hearts.

Many things in our lives make promises. Some promise to give us pleasure, thrills, status, or escape from pain. We hear voices whispering or shouting these promises all the time. Conversations at work or with friends, ads on television and billboards, and other forms of communication promise to fulfill our dreams. All these things are like competing hawkers at a flea market, trying to convince us to come to their tents to buy what they're selling.

But we can choose only one thing.

Amid the din of all these voices, we have to listen hard to hear another voice that says, "I am the way, the truth, and the life" and offers us an adventure and an abundant life—if we allow this to be our one thing.

Identify some of the competing voices and their promises in your life.

What have you had in your box in the past year or so? What are you putting in your box now?

See John 14:6.

LIFE PROMISES

[I am] confident of this very thing, that
He who has begun a good work in you
will complete it until the day of Jesus
Christ.
PHILIPPIANS 1:6

In the way of righteousness is life,
And in its pathway there is no death.
PROVERBS 12:28

Seek first the kingdom of God and His
righteousness, and all these things shall
be added to you.
MATTHEW 6:33

A WORK IN PROGRESS

THE MOMENT WE TRUST IN CHRIST, some amazing transformations take place. All our sins are forgiven, we join God's family, we receive eternal life, and God's Spirit takes up residence inside us. These things are wonderful truths of our new life in Christ, but we've only begun to let those things sink deeply into our lives to change our motivations, thoughts, and habits. We are works in progress, and we'll remain unfinished until we see Jesus face-to-face.

As we consider this fact, two important principles emerge: First, we shouldn't expect perfection. We have much to learn on our journey, and we need to unpack the distortions, bad habits, and selfish attitudes we carry in our backpacks. Second, we aren't on this path alone. God has committed Himself to be our guide all along the way. He is helping us unload some of the excess baggage we carry, and He gives us directions when we come to a crossroads.

The trail is long, but if we stick with it, our journey with Jesus will be the greatest thrill of our lives!

How does it help you to know that you're a work in progress?

What do you need to do to walk more closely with God on the journey?

The refining pot is for silver and the
  furnace for gold,
 And a man is valued by what others
  say of him.
PROVERBS 27:21

Humble yourselves under the mighty
hand of God, that He may exalt you in
due time.
1 PETER 5:6

Commit your way to the LORD,
 Trust also in Him,
 And He shall bring it to pass.
PSALM 37:5

REFINING
YOUR REPUTATION

OUR REPUTATIONS occasionally may be unfairly tarnished when others spread gossip that's not true, but over time, the judgment of public opinion rings fairly true. That can be good news or bad news, depending on the opinion!

When precious metals endure the refining process, ore is heated to the melting point. At intervals, the dross, or sludge, is skimmed from the top, gradually leaving the purified metal. In the same way, the opinions of others are the fire in our lives to separate the noble from the selfish. If we are wise, bad reports can be tremendously valuable—if we'll accept them and respond with changes. But if we take ourselves off the fire by excusing our actions and blaming someone else, we won't learn, and we won't benefit from the heat of criticism.

A good reputation takes time to earn, just as it takes time for gold and silver to purify. Stay in the heat, learn hard lessons, and let God use the fires of others' opinions to purify your heart.

How do you respond to criticism?

Who are the people you trust to tell you the truth?

LIFE PROMISES

The things that you have heard from me among many witnesses, commit these to faithful men who will be able to teach others also.

2 TIMOTHY 2:2

Let no corrupt word proceed out of your mouth, but what is good for necessary edification, that it may impart grace to the hearers.

EPHESIANS 4:29

Take heed to yourself and to the doctrine. Continue in them, for in doing this you will save both yourself and those who hear you.

1 TIMOTHY 4:16

PASS IT ON

WE MAY THINK we invented viral marketing, but Paul used it almost two millennia ago. Viral marketing occurs when a product or service generates enough enthusiasm to cause people to tell their friends and business associates about the product or service. The life-changing truth about Christ works the same way.

Paul invested tremendous resources in Timothy. In every kind of circumstance, Paul taught and modeled the truth for Timothy. He told Timothy to pass along everything he had learned, but not just to anybody. He carefully instructed Timothy to select "faithful men" who have the heart and the skills to teach others. These men would then do the same thing, selecting great leaders and imparting God's truth to them, and they'd do the same with people they selected.

Throughout the world, people who become believers are won because men and women have caught the "virus" from faithful, skilled, passionate men and women who were "infected" by others. Today, most of us can look back at a generation or two of faithful people who, like Paul and Timothy, were part of the viral marketing of the Christian faith.

Why is it important to select faithful people to invest our time in?

How are you doing in imparting the faith to faithful people? Explain your answer.

LIFE PROMISES

He who walks with wise men will
        be wise,
    But the companion of fools will
        be destroyed.
PROVERBS 13:20

The fear of the Lord is the beginning
        of wisdom;
    A good understanding have
        all those who do His
        commandments.
PSALM 111:10

With Him are wisdom and strength,
    He has counsel and understanding.
JOB 12:13

WALK WITH THE WISE

WE SEE IT ALL THE TIME: Teenagers join the "wrong crowd," and they make dumb choices they never would have made before. Sometimes these choices are minor, but sometimes they're fatal. The choice of friends isn't important just for teenagers; it's crucial for all of us.

Why are some of us attracted to "fools"? In many cases, it's because they seem to live exciting lives. They take risks and they laugh, play, and sing loudly. This life looks like fun. Many of us are wired to enjoy taking risks, and fools take more risks than others. The rush of adrenaline can be addictive.

On the other hand, "wise people" sometimes have a bad reputation. Actually, we often mistakenly believe *boring*, *stiff*, *religious*, and *self-righteous* are words that describe wisdom, and that doesn't make wisdom attractive at all! True wisdom, though, is the ability to really live, to squeeze every drop of meaning out of life, and to look to God to give us the greatest adventure life has to offer. Can you find a wise friend or two? Can you be one? That's your challenge.

What are some other reasons fools can be so attractive to so many people?

How would you describe a really wise person?

LIFE PROMISES

He who tills his land will be satisfied
        with bread,
    But he who follows frivolity is
        devoid of understanding.
PROVERBS 12:11

The righteous shall flourish like
        a palm tree,
    He shall grow like a cedar in
        Lebanon.
PSALM 92:12

A person is a fool to store up earthly
wealth but not have a rich relationship
with God.
LUKE 12:21, NLT

PROSPERITY THEOLOGY—REALLY!

EVERYWHERE WE LOOK, we see the incredible wealth of our culture. In some Christian circles, leaders have adopted the desire for more possessions and pleasure, and they promise their followers that God wants them to have even more stuff.

Does God want us to prosper? Yes, but God's primary benchmark for prosperity is that we love Him so much that all other desires pale in comparison. Jesus taught that true fulfillment comes from "losing our lives" in our affection and obedience to God, not by acquiring more possessions and enjoying more pleasures.

Material possessions and health are desires but they aren't rights, and God doesn't promise them. We can expect spiritual prosperity as we follow Christ, but we shouldn't demand that God give us the prosperity the world values.

We can have the utmost confidence that God uses every circumstance in our lives to deepen our love for Him and make our souls prosper, but we should hold our desires far more loosely.

What happens in our hearts when we demand worldly prosperity?

What are some adjustments you need to make to refocus your heart on true prosperity?

See Mark 8:35.

LIFE PROMISES

Let no one despise your youth, but be
an example to the believers in word,
in conduct, in love, in spirit, in faith,
in purity.
1 TIMOTHY 4:12

Whatever you want men to do to you,
do also to them, for this is the Law and
the Prophets.
MATTHEW 7:12

We . . . do not cease to pray for you,
and to ask that you may be filled
with the knowledge of His will in all
wisdom and spiritual understanding;
. . . strengthened with all might,
according to His glorious power, for all
patience and longsuffering with joy.
COLOSSIANS 1:9, 11

LEAD BY EXAMPLE

GOD HAS GIVEN ALL OF US skills and talents, but He is more interested in the character of the man or woman who uses these abilities. Others will watch how we treat our spouses and children and our fellow employees, how we respond to annoying people and difficult situations, and how we talk about corporate executives when they make poor decisions.

When a Christian goes out of his or her way to care for someone who is hurting, overlooks petty offenses and takes steps to resolve big ones, finds something else to do when the rest of the team goes to a strip club, and exudes a positive attitude while being ruthlessly honest about difficulties—people notice!

All of us have a hundred choices to make each day. We may not recognize many of them because we're so steeped in habitual attitudes and behaviors, but we have constant opportunities to demonstrate love or selfishness, faith or doubt, hope or complaints, purity or sinful passion. If we choose to be Christ's examples to those around us, we're in for a great ride of seeing Him touch people through us.

Who is the best "leader by example" you know? Describe that person's impact on others.

What new choices do you need to make, and what new habits do you need to develop?

LIFE PROMISES

If any of you lacks wisdom, let him ask of God, who gives to all liberally and without reproach, and it will be given to him.
JAMES 1:5

[Jesus said,] "Whoever hears these sayings of Mine, and does them, I will liken him to a wise man who built his house on the rock: and the rain descended, the floods came, and the winds blew and beat on that house; and it did not fall, for it was founded on the rock."
MATTHEW 7:24-25

Turn at my rebuke;
>   Surely I will pour out my spirit
>   on you;
>   I will make my words known
>   to you.

PROVERBS 1:23

HAVING THE WISDOM TO ASK FOR WISDOM

CORPORATIONS HIRE CONSULTANTS for any and all management needs, and executive coaches assist leaders to take steps forward in their personal lives and careers. We want feedback, we want the infusion of new ideas, and we want accountability. These are exactly what God promises if we'll just ask Him for them.

When a problem comes along, we read books, call friends, and scour the Internet for articles related to our need. We expect this approach from those who don't know Christ, but Christians have the greatest resource the universe has ever known: God Himself!

Certainly, we can learn a lot from seminars and books, from workshops, and from experts. But our first, most important, and most powerful source of wisdom is God. He is just waiting for us to turn to Him, to express our need, to search the Scriptures, and to invite His Spirit to guide us.

When we hire a consultant, we receive a promise for services to be rendered. God's promise is that He will pour out His wisdom "liberally" when we ask and without condemning us for getting into trouble in the first place.

How is God's promise to give us wisdom like and unlike hiring a consultant or coach?

How do you need God's wisdom to guide you today?

LIFE PROMISES

O LORD,
> You are our Father;
> We are the clay, and You our potter;
> And all we are the work of Your
> > hand.

ISAIAH 64:8

The precious sons of Zion,
> Valuable as fine gold,
> How they are regarded as clay pots,
> The work of the hands of the potter!

LAMENTATIONS 4:2

I [Jeremiah] did as [the Lord] told me and found the potter working at his wheel. But the jar he was making did not turn out as he had hoped, so he . . . started over.

JEREMIAH 18:3-4, NLT

STARTING OVER

THE BIBLE and he history of people of faith give us a rich record of God's not giving up on us when we fail. Abraham was a coward, but God transformed him into the father of our faith. Jacob was a deceiver, but God touched him and made him the father of the twelve tribes. Peter denied Jesus, but a few days after the Resurrection, Jesus met him to reaffirm his acceptance, and Peter became the leader of the early church. The list of men and women who started over is almost endless.

God works diligently to form us into useful, beautiful vessels, but sometimes things don't work out. It's not the potter's fault; a flaw in the clay causes the problem. But that doesn't hinder God. He lovingly starts over, eliminating the flaw and adding the elements of the Spirit, the accountability of friends, and the guidance of the Word to start shaping us again. When God starts over with us, we may not become instantly useful. It takes time; however, sooner or later we'll be useful again.

What kinds of flaws can make us unusable to the Potter?

What's your role and what's God's role in shaping you?

LIFE PROMISES

The King will answer and say to them,
"Assuredly, I say to you, inasmuch as
you did it to one of the least of these
My brethren, you did it to Me."
MATTHEW 25:40

Let no one seek his own, but each one
the other's well-being.
1 CORINTHIANS 10:24

You, brethren, have been called to
liberty; only do not use liberty as an
opportunity for the flesh, but through
love serve one another.
GALATIANS 5:13

THE LEAST OF THESE

OUTWARD APPEARANCE can be a sham. God cares far more about the content of our hearts and the expression of our hearts in loving actions. One of the clearest windows on the condition of our hearts, Jesus said, is how we treat "the least of these" around us.

Who are these people? They are the ones most of us ignore. We move to the suburbs to get away from them. If they *do* get in our way, we pass by as quickly as possible. Avoiding them, though, isn't what pleases Jesus. He values those of us who see needs and take steps to meet them. The needs of nice, clean people? Yes, but also the needs of those who are dirty, lonely, hurting; who are outcasts; and who can't give anything in return. We show our devotion to Christ when we feed the hungry, give a drink to those who are thirsty, invite strangers to our homes, clothe those who wear rags, and visit the sick and the prisoners.

Who are some needy people you see every day? Do you need to leave a cocoon of safety and peace to be with them?

What is one new habit you can develop to care for needy people?

See 1 Samuel 16:7.

LIFE PROMISES

Ask, and it will be given to you; seek, and you will find; knock, and it will be opened to you. For everyone who asks receives, and he who seeks finds, and to him who knocks it will be opened.

MATTHEW 7:7-8

Patient endurance is what you need now, so that you will continue to do God's will. Then you will receive all that he has promised.

HEBREWS 10:36, NLT

Through God we will do valiantly.

PSALM 60:12

THANK GOD FOR A SECOND CHANCE

MOSES WAS ONE OF THE GREATEST LEADERS the world has ever known. We often think of him as the man who led God's people out of slavery in Egypt. But that's only part of his story.

Moses had murdered an Egyptian. His motive may have been to help his people, but murder is murder. God sent him to the middle of nowhere for forty long, lonely years. During all that time, how often did he think his life was over? Did he despair that his life would never have meaning again?

But God gave him a second chance. It didn't come when Moses wanted or expected it, but when it came, he responded. Many of us have blown it in a big way, either at work or at home, publicly or privately. We've experienced the consequences of our sins, and we feel like we've been exiled to a foreign land. Yet, God is amazingly gracious. We don't deserve a second chance, but He gives it—and maybe a third and a fourth, too. We may wait for a long time, but when it comes, we need to be ready to respond.

Whom do you know who feels exiled and needs a second chance?

What are some ways we can be ready to respond when the second chance comes?

See Exodus 2–3.

 ## LIFE PROMISES

There are many plans in a man's heart,
    Nevertheless the Lord's counsel—
        that will stand.
PROVERBS 19:21

Be strong and of good courage, and
do it; do not fear nor be dismayed,
for the Lord God—my God—will be
with you. He will not leave you nor
forsake you.
1 CHRONICLES 28:20

Comfort each other and edify one
another, just as you also are doing.
1 THESSALONIANS 5:11

SUCCESSION PLANNING

EVEN AMONG COMMITTED CHRISTIANS, disagreements can cause divisions and necessitate a change in plans. Paul and Barnabas established churches throughout the Eastern Mediterranean. On one of their trips, they took along John Mark, but he deserted Paul at a critical point. Barnabas wanted to give the young man a second chance, but Paul disagreed.

The question here wasn't between right and wrong. Was taking John Mark along again a risk? Yes. Was Barnabas gracious to offer him a second chance? Certainly. The two men, though, couldn't agree, so they parted ways.

Leadership sometimes demands hard choices. Different leaders have different perspectives. They can try to come to an agreement, but at the end of the day, someone has to make a decision so the work can move ahead. Sometimes the original plan does not work out, but God always has a solution. He often has plans that we never considered.

Don't be afraid of disagreements. State your opinion and try to find common ground, but realize that God may have other plans.

Would you have given John Mark a second chance? Why or why not?

What ground rules and expectations should be put in place when Christians disagree?

See Acts 15:36-39.

 **LIFE PROMISES**

Honor all people. Love the brotherhood. Fear God. Honor the king.
1 PETER 2:17

Glory, honor, and peace to everyone who works what is good.
ROMANS 2:10

Bear one another's burdens, and so fulfill the law of Christ. For if anyone thinks himself to be something, when he is nothing, he deceives himself.
GALATIANS 6:2-3

DON'T FOOL YOURSELF

WHEN WE ARE INVOLVED in leading people or helping the disadvantaged, we can lose track of our motives. Controlling people is heady stuff. We feel powerful, and we can feel indispensable.

Paul reminds us not to fool ourselves. Humility is essential in leading and helping so that we don't let power go to our heads. Instead of being distracted by the abilities and positions of others, we need to stop and examine only our own work and our own hearts. The measuring stick isn't that we know more than other people or that we have more power than others. The measuring stick is Christ, who "emptied Himself" to serve.

Comparing may be a natural thing everybody does, but people in leadership need to avoid it at all costs because it feeds insecurity or pride, not humility and trust in God. On the day we stand before Christ, He won't ask us if we were more powerful than others. He'll ask only if we did all we could to help, serve, and give, taking responsibility for our choices—all to "fulfill the law of Christ" by helping others instead of wielding power for our own sake.

What roles do you have that can foster comparison with others?

What would it look like to "fulfill the law of Christ" in each of these roles?

See Philippians 2:2, 7.

LIFE PROMISES

I [Paul] exhort first of all that supplications, prayers, intercessions, and giving of thanks be made for all men, for kings and all who are in authority, that we may lead a quiet and peaceable life in all godliness and reverence. For this is good and acceptable in the sight of God our Savior.

1 TIMOTHY 2:1-3

No other foundation can anyone lay than that which is laid, which is Jesus Christ.

1 CORINTHIANS 3:11

We urge you, brethren, to recognize those who labor among you, and are over you in the Lord and admonish you, and to esteem them very highly in love for their work's sake. Be at peace among yourselves.

1 THESSALONIANS 5:12-13

PRAYING FOR LEADERS

IT'S EASY TO COMPLAIN about national politicians, corporate managers, bureaucrats at every level of government, and church leaders, but instead, Paul tells us to pray for them! Paul has a very broad view in mind. Good governance provides peace and stability so that the gospel can be spread unhindered to people next door and to the most remote parts of the earth. When our attention and resources aren't absorbed by wars, bickering, and conflict, we can invest our energies in the things that really matter.

Paul didn't suggest that we agree with all politicians. His eyes were fixed on an invisible Kingdom where God reigns and where grace and forgiveness are the highest virtues. The reality of life in this world is that we can get caught up completely in the things that are seen but neglect the things that are unseen. Political power can serve the Kingdom by providing peace and stability. Then we can focus on what matters most.

Whenever you think of our political, corporate, and religious leaders, pray for them, for the peace they can provide, and for the gospel to spread under the umbrella of their authority.

How do you usually think and talk about your political, corporate, and religious leaders?

Take some time now to pray for them and for the cause of Christ to spread.

LIFE PROMISES

[The Lord said,] "I will give you
shepherds according to My heart,
who will feed you with knowledge and
understanding."
JEREMIAH 3:15

Listen to counsel and receive
         instruction,
    That you may be wise in your
         latter days.
PROVERBS 19:20

Receive my instruction, and not silver,
    And knowledge rather than choice
         gold.
PROVERBS 8:10

LEADERS ARE LEARNERS

ONE OF THE MOST ATTRACTIVE TRAITS of a powerful leader is getting excited about learning a new skill or gaining fresh insights. Conversely, one of the most discouraging characteristics of some in leadership is a know-it-all mentality that walls them off from new ideas. Leaders who love to learn add enthusiasm and creativity to every meeting and every relationship, and they are great examples to others in the organization.

Spiritual life, like all aspects of life and leadership, requires a rigorous commitment to learning and growing. When we stop growing, our momentum quickly fades. The Christian life is often called a walk. A slow, steady, consistent pursuit of God and His will will characterize our lives. And, like the roots of a tree, we reach down deep into the truth and grace of God to find nourishment. Soaking up sustenance never stops, and even in times of drought, we find sources of strength if we've gone deep enough. And finally, like a sturdy building, each choice we make to honor God is a block in the structure of our spiritual experience.

We grow stronger with each God-honoring decision.

What happens to us when we stop learning?

What are you doing right now to keep walking, going deeper, and growing stronger?

 **LIFE PROMISES**

When [Uzziah] was strong his heart was lifted up, to his destruction, for he transgressed against the LORD his God.
2 CHRONICLES 26:16

Pride goes before destruction,
    And a haughty spirit before a fall.
PROVERBS 16:18

I [Paul] have reason to glory in Christ Jesus in the things which pertain to God. For I will not dare to speak of any of those things which Christ has not accomplished through me.
ROMANS 15:17-18

KNOCKED DOWN

GREAT LEADERS often have great pride. To become useful to God, their pride has to be crushed. God can then use the broken pieces to create new, humble people whose consummate abilities are under the leading of the Spirit instead of being driven by selfish ambition.

For example, Saul, who later became known as Paul, was a member of the religious elite of Israel. Saul was thoroughly convinced he was always right.

On the road to Damascus, God met Saul in a blinding light. Saul realized that all he had believed was false and that his life had been a lie. That moment was the pivotal point in this strong leader's life. He was literally and figuratively knocked down. His pride was shattered, and his confidence blown away. But he submitted himself to Christ and to Christ's gospel, and God rebuilt him to become the most influential leader the church has ever known.

When God knocks you down, don't shake your fist at Him. Instead, let God reform your passions and redirect your path so that you can use all your God-given abilities for Him and for others instead of for yourself.

How can you tell if it's God who's knocking you down?

Does it encourage you or depress you that God is willing to crush your pride to reform you?

See Acts 9:1-31.

Let all those rejoice who put their trust
    in You;
    Let them ever shout for joy, because
        You defend them;
    Let those also who love Your name
    Be joyful in You.

PSALM 5:11

The grass withers and the flowers fade,
    but the word of our God stands
        forever.

ISAIAH 40:8, NLT

O Lord of hosts,
    Blessed is the man who trusts in You!

PSALM 84:12

TRUST IS A MUST

SOMETIMES, THE STRESSES AND STRUGGLES of life take their toll on our emotions and our outlook. We never intend for it to happen, but our sense of joy is washed away in a sea of demands and conflicts. King David experienced the pressures of leadership, but even in the middle of these pressures, he found great joy in his relationship with God.

To David, God wasn't just a cosmic principle or a distant deity to be worshiped during certain times of the week in order to conform his life to a religious pattern. No, God was a person—a wonderful, trustworthy person he could delight in. David deeply appreciated God's deliverance and His wisdom. In reply to God's personal intervention and care, David voiced the response of all believers who are thrilled with God: We "shout for joy"!

Our task is to turn our struggles into steps toward God instead of away from Him. We all experience difficulties at home and at work, but if we turn our gaze toward God, we'll find Him to be a rock we can stand on in those times of stress.

Whom do you know whose relationship with God becomes stronger during times of struggle?

What about God's love, care, and provision causes you to shout for joy?

LIFE PROMISES

I [Paul] have shown you in every way, by laboring like this, that you must support the weak. And remember the words of the Lord Jesus, that He said, "It is more blessed to give than to receive."
ACTS 20:35

If you extend your soul to the hungry
    And satisfy the afflicted soul,
    Then your light shall dawn in
        the darkness,
    And your darkness shall be as
        the noonday.
ISAIAH 58:10

[Jesus said,] "Whoever gives one of these little ones only a cup of cold water in the name of a disciple, assuredly, I say to you, he shall by no means lose his reward."
MATTHEW 10:42

GIVING IS LIVING

OUR CULTURE, like every culture throughout history, is remarkably self-absorbed. Selfishness transcends time, race, and societies. But because we have more disposable income than any other people in history, we have more that we can spend to indulge ourselves. Though we claim to be shrewd, we are all infected by at least a light case of consumerism, and we clutch things more tightly than we should.

The promise of advertising is that the product or service will give us fulfillment in our lives! People who have walked with God for a while understand the danger in this lie. We know that having more stuff fills us for only a short time, and soon we thirst for even more. And we know that we *really live* only when we *really give.* Heartfelt fulfillment comes when we pour out our lives to help those who can never invite us to a dinner party, take us out on their boat, or make us look good in any way. When we help the weak, the poor, and the sick—expecting nothing in return—we are most like God, and He blesses us beyond anything the world can offer.

What act of giving or service has brought you the most joy?

In what way is it really "more blessed to give than to receive"?

LIFE PROMISES

A friend loves at all times,
   And a brother is born for adversity.
PROVERBS 17:17

Be kind to one another, tenderhearted,
forgiving one another, even as God in
Christ forgave you.
EPHESIANS 4:32

Do not forsake your own friend or
   your father's friend.
PROVERBS 27:10

THE VALUE OF FRIENDSHIP

JOE HAD SEEN his comfortable, stable, happy life crumble over the last few months. Demands of his in-laws created tension with his wife, and the tension continued to escalate. He noticed that his circle of friends gradually diminished. It seemed that few of them wanted to hang around somebody who wasn't much fun anymore.

"I've never felt so lonely in my life," he reported later. "I thought they'd all leave, but Phil stayed. When I was at my worst, he didn't walk away. You have no idea what that meant—and still means—to me."

All significant relationships are tested by disputes and difficulties. It's easy to walk away when friends no longer give as much as they take, but a true friend moves toward someone who is hurting. He or she provides stability when life is out of control and a listening ear when no one else wants to understand. A true friend doesn't jump in to fix problems. He or she offers advice sparingly.

We all want friends like this. To *have* a friend who cares about us during difficult times, we need to *be* this kind of friend.

In your life, who has been this kind of friend?

Who needs you to be this kind of friend today? What will you do to show support?

LIFE PROMISES

Behold, how good and how pleasant
    it is
  For brethren to dwell together
    in unity!
PSALM 133:1

There is one body and one Spirit, just
as you were called in one hope of your
calling.
EPHESIANS 4:4

I [Paul] plead with you, brethren, by the
name of our Lord Jesus Christ, that you
all speak the same thing, and that there
be no divisions among you, but that
you be perfectly joined together in the
same mind and in the same judgment.
1 CORINTHIANS 1:10

UNITY IN ACTION

WE'VE ALL HEARD STORIES of organizations, companies, and churches that disintegrated into bitter conflict. Quite often, the conflict began with gossip, envy, fierce competition that produced genuine bitterness, or someone shifting blame for a failure. Whatever the cause, people took their eyes off the common goal and started protecting themselves. That's no way to build a team!

But unity isn't the goal. Rather, unity is a result, one of a shared vision and cooperative efforts. In families, companies, churches, or any other organization, leaders can build unity by living for and pointing people toward a purpose that transcends each individual. With that goal in mind, they can identify and affirm each person's abilities and contributions, overlook petty issues, and communicate with clarity and compassion. When each person feels valued and included, incredible things can happen!

What's the temperature of your family or organization? If you aren't "dwelling together in unity," don't try to force it. Instead, focus your energies on clarifying a purpose and enlisting cooperation to achieve a common goal. It'll make a difference in those around you . . . and in you.

Describe the climate in your family, company, church, or other organization.

What can you do to clarify the purpose and enlist cooperation?

LIFE PROMISES

[The Lord] said to me, "My grace is sufficient for you, for My strength is made perfect in weakness." Therefore most gladly I [Paul] will rather boast in my infirmities, that the power of Christ may rest upon me.
2 CORINTHIANS 12:9

I bow my knees to the Father of our Lord Jesus Christ . . . that He would grant you, according to the riches of His glory, to be strengthened with might through His Spirit in the inner man, that Christ may dwell in your hearts through faith.
EPHESIANS 3:14, 16-17

I can do all things through Christ who strengthens me.
PHILIPPIANS 4:13

ALWAYS SUFFICIENT

ONE OF THE HARDEST LESSONS for most of us to learn is that our points of weakness can become our greatest opportunities to experience God's strength. Too often, we deny we're weak and we miss wonderful steps of growth.

When Corrie ten Boom was a young woman growing up under Nazi domination, she told her father, "I'm not sure I can survive the strain."

Her father, a wise man, asked her, "Corrie, when you take the bus home each day, does the driver ask for a year's fare?"

"No, Father," she replied.

"Does he ask you for a week's fare?"

"No, Father, he doesn't. I only give him the fare for that ride."

Her father's eyes brightened, and he explained, "That's the way God's grace is for us. He always gives us what we need at the time we need it."

From time to time, all of us face situations when we feel submerged in confusion, pain, and difficulties. At those moments, we don't need grace and wisdom for the whole solution. We just need them for the next step. God will give us exactly what we need at the time we need it.

How have you seen God's strength demonstrated when someone admitted his or her weakness?

Is there a situation in your life right now in which you need God's strength? In what way are you weak?

Blessed are the peacemakers,
> For they shall be called sons of God.

MATTHEW 5:9

Do not be conformed to this world, but be transformed by the renewing of your mind, that you may prove what is that good and acceptable and perfect will of God.

ROMANS 12:2

In all things we commend ourselves as ministers of God.

2 CORINTHIANS 6:4

BUILDING BRIDGES

CONFLICT IS SO COMMON in our culture that we barely notice it anymore. But simmering anger soon turns into destructive bitterness, hatred, and the desire to take revenge, which destroy relationships.

In conflict, some of us clench our fists, raise our voices, make demands, and try to intimidate people. Others look down to avoid eye contact, barely mumble above a whisper, and give in to stop the argument. Neither of these responses to conflict builds bridges of trust and understanding.

A peacemaker is someone who treasures relationships based on mutual respect and works hard to help people take steps in that direction. In some cases, a simple misunderstanding can be resolved fairly easily, but long-standing, deep wounds take time and attention to heal. Gradually, suspicion turns to understanding, and bitterness gives way to forgiveness.

When we've benefited from a peacemaker who stepped in to build a bridge between us and someone we've despised, we are amazed and grateful for the peacemaker's work. Peacemakers are, indeed, "sons of God," who follow the pattern of the Prince of Peace by offering hope, trust, and relief to people whose relationships have been shredded by hatred.

How has conflict affected your stress levels, your happiness, and your relationships?

Where and how might you be a peacemaker to build bridges between people in conflict?

LIFE PROMISES

Be still, and know that I am God;
        I will be exalted among the nations,
        I will be exalted in the earth!
PSALM 46:10

You will guide me with Your counsel,
        And afterward receive me to glory.
PSALM 73:24

Whatever things were written before
were written for our learning, that we
through the patience and comfort of
the Scriptures might have hope.
ROMANS 15:4

BE STILL

IN THE MIDST OF TURMOIL, God speaks to us and calmly says, "Be still, and know that I am God." The Lord doesn't run around trying to fix everything, and He doesn't direct us to work like crazy to make everything right. Work might come later, but before it does, we need God's perspective. And the only way to get it is to stop, look, listen, and remember the goodness and greatness of Almighty God. When the time is right, God's grace and strength will be evident.

Modern society produces tremendous stress. Expectations are sky-high, and opportunities quickly morph into demands for more things, better opportunities, and higher achievements. Some of our stresses come from outside, but we create many others. Whatever the source, God stands in the midst of our chaotic lives. When everything seems to be coming unglued, He whispers, "Stop. Be still. Listen to me, and be sure that I can do anything that needs to be done." Will we listen?

Describe a time when you felt like your life was coming unglued.

How does it help to stop, be still, and focus on God in times of chaos?

He gives power to the weak,
    And to those who have no might He
        increases strength.
ISAIAH 40:29

[David said,] "I will sing of Your power;
    Yes, I will sing aloud of Your mercy
        in the morning;
    For You have been my defense
    And refuge in the day of my trouble."
PSALM 59:16

A bruised reed He will not break,
    And smoking flax He will not
        quench,
    Till He sends forth justice
        to victory.
MATTHEW 12:20

INCREASE YOUR POWER

THE CHRISTIAN LIFE—and especially the nature of spiritual growth—is a paradox: To grow strong, we have to admit our weaknesses. Most people spend their lives trying to avoid weakness in every area of life, and when they feel most vulnerable, they try to act powerful to fool people. For those who follow Christ, though, the unwillingness to admit weakness is a serious flaw that short-circuits God's transforming power. Honesty about our weaknesses may threaten us, but it opens the door to God's liberating truth, stunning freedom, and real change.

We can learn the habit of being honest with God about our weaknesses, but most of us are honest only in a crisis. At a point where we have tried everything else and failed, we're finally ready to admit we need God's help. We admit we are weak, and we trust in God's guidance and strength. When the crisis is over, though, many of us go back to trusting in ourselves. Real growth comes when we can admit, every day, "Lord, I need your wisdom and strength in my situations today. Please help me." And He will.

How is admitting our weaknesses the doorway to experiencing God's strength?

What are some areas of weakness in your life today?

LIFE PROMISES

We love Him because He first loved us. If someone says, "I love God," and hates his brother, he is a liar; for he who does not love his brother whom he has seen, how can he love God whom he has not seen? And this commandment we have from Him: that he who loves God must love his brother also.

1 JOHN 4:19-21

Surely goodness and mercy shall
    follow me
  All the days of my life;
  And I will dwell in the house
    of the Lord
  Forever.

PSALM 23:6

You also have become dead to the law through the body of Christ, that you may be married to another—to Him who was raised from the dead, that we should bear fruit to God.

ROMANS 7:4

REACHING OUT

SOME PEOPLE ANNOY US. They interrupt us when we're trying to concentrate, ignore us when we need their help, or give us unwanted advice. Sometimes, the best we can do is to tolerate them.

Tolerating people, however, isn't loving them, and God has set a high standard for us in relationships. God has imparted genuine, unconditional love to us, and He gives us an example of what love looks like. He is the prime mover, the One who initiated love toward us when we were completely unlovable.

The love we show others indicates our level of love for God. If we fail to love horizontally, we can assume there's a problem in our vertical relationship with God. We won't reach out in love until God has first reached into our hearts to enable us to love Him.

We love those around us by pursuing what's best for them. When we're listening, we're fully present in the moment. When we're caring, we give everything we've got because we're aware that God gave His all to us. The more we experience the transforming love of God, the more His love spills out of us toward those around us.

Who are the people and what are the situations when the best you can do is to tolerate them?

How can you experience God's love more deeply? What difference will it make?

Whatever things are true, whatever
things are noble, whatever things are
just, whatever things are pure, whatever
things are lovely, whatever things are
of good report, if there is any virtue
and if there is anything praiseworthy—
meditate on these things.

PHILIPPIANS 4:8

All of you be of one mind, having
compassion for one another; love
as brothers, be tenderhearted, be
courteous.

1 PETER 3:8

Let us pursue the things which make
for peace and the things by which one
may edify another.

ROMANS 14:19

WHATEVER!

IF OUR BRAINS ARE THE OPERATING SYSTEM, our thought patterns are the software our minds run on. To some degree, the software in all our minds is corrupted. We have trouble thinking correctly, so we get prideful in the good times and fearful in the bad.

Right thinking is a skill all of us can learn, even though our software will always have glitches in it until the day we see Jesus face-to-face. Focusing our minds on noble things and giving thanks can become habits as we practice them more and more, but negative, destructive, selfish thoughts creep in from time to time. When we find ourselves heading down the wrong thought trail, we don't need to beat ourselves up about it—we're only human; however, we can take definitive action to focus our minds again on whatever is true, noble, and praiseworthy. We may not be able to completely eliminate unhealthy thoughts, but we can act quickly to replace them. As Martin Luther said, "We can't keep birds from flying over our heads, but we can keep them from building nests in our hair!"

How would you assess the effectiveness of your mental software?

What are some practical things you can do to replace negative thoughts with positive ones?

LIFE PROMISES

Not what goes into the mouth defiles a man; but what comes out of the mouth, this defiles a man.

MATTHEW 15:11

Let the words of my mouth and the
meditation of my heart
Be acceptable in Your sight,
O Lord, my strength and my
Redeemer.

PSALM 19:14

The mouth of the righteous brings
forth wisdom,
But the perverse tongue will be
cut out.

PROVERBS 10:31

THE WELL OF THE HEART

IN JESUS' DAY, people were more particular about foods than a conference of dieters! They had rules about what you could eat and what you couldn't eat, and they had rules about the rules. They were convinced that the food people ate could bless them or ruin them, but Jesus turned their thinking upside down. He told them that what goes into their mouths isn't as important as what comes out of them.

Most of us think very little about our communication. We've developed habits of saying the same things in the same ways to the same people. However, we need to be more intentional about the words we say to one another. Healing messages say, "I love you," "I'm proud of you," and "You're really good at that!" Critical words cut like a knife. And sarcasm is the same knife with a pearl handle.

Words reveal what's in our hearts. If what spills out is too often negative, biting, caustic, or sarcastic, we need to ask God to fill the well with faith, hope, and love so that positive words come out by the bucketful.

Think of the conversations you've had in the past day. How would you describe the content of your words?

What changes do you need to make in your communication, especially with those you love?

LIFE PROMISES

Wait on the LORD;
>   Be of good courage,
>   And He shall strengthen your heart;
>   Wait, I say, on the LORD!

PSALM 27:14

Multitudes, multitudes in the valley
>   of decision!
>   For the day of the LORD is near in
>   the valley of decision.

JOEL 3:14

Our citizenship is in heaven, from
which we also eagerly wait for the
Savior, the Lord Jesus Christ.

PHILIPPIANS 3:20

WAITING

WAITING IS INCREDIBLY DIFFICULT. Author and pastor Charles Swindoll says it's the hardest thing Christians have to do. Because we live in an instant society, we're not used to waiting for anything. But God uses the discipline of waiting to teach us lessons we can't learn any other way.

Sometimes God puts the brakes on our plans because He wants to teach us an important lesson and He has to get our attention. Occasionally, God puts up a stop sign to keep us from going in a certain direction. Quite often, we're so sure we're headed the right way that we won't listen unless He stops us dead in our tracks. Of course, we sometimes need God to grab us and stop the runaway train of our lives because we've sinned and we need to repent.

To us, waiting seems like a waste—or worse, it feels like things will never be right again. When we have to wait, we shouldn't just sit and fritter away the time. We should pursue God with all our hearts, try to determine the reason God wants us to wait, and trust His goodness and timing because He is, after all, God.

Describe the last time you experienced waiting for God to act.

Which of the reasons above might have been God's purpose in this experience?

LIFE PROMISES

Let your conduct be without covetousness; be content with such things as you have. For He Himself has said, "I will never leave you nor forsake you."
HEBREWS 13:5

If you lend money to any of My people who are poor among you, you shall not be like a moneylender to him; you shall not charge him interest.
EXODUS 22:25

He who loves silver will not be satisfied
        with silver;
    Nor he who loves abundance, with
        increase.
    This also is vanity.
ECCLESIASTES 5:10

KNOW WHAT YOU'VE GOT

WANTING WHAT OTHERS HAVE comes from either insecurity or greed. When we feel insecure, we check out what others have, what they wear, what they drive, where they go on vacation, and all other external measuring sticks. On the other hand, we may just be greedy and want more than what we have. Either way, craving things steals our hearts and ruins relationships.

The writer to the Hebrews tells us to recognize coveting, no matter what its cause, and get rid of it, replacing it with a deep sense of contentment. Where does the contentment come from? From acknowledging that everything we have and everything we are come from God. For our hearts to be filled with His grace and strength, we don't need anything else. True contentment comes from a rich, real relationship with Christ. He promises to be as near as our breath, and He'll never leave us for a second.

A craving for things reveals an empty—or at least a partially empty—heart, one that can be filled and overflowing with the presence of our King, Savior, and Best Friend.

How much do you crave things? What do you hope they'll do for you?

In what way does Christ's presence give us true contentment?

LIFE PROMISES

The labor of the righteous leads to life,
    The wages of the wicked to sin.
PROVERBS 10:16

When you eat the labor of your hands,
    You shall be happy, and it shall be
        well with you.
PSALM 128:2

Every man should eat and drink and
enjoy the good of all his labor—it is
the gift of God.
ECCLESIASTES 3:13

GOOD WORK

FOR ALL OF US, finding a good "fit" in our work has multiple benefits. When our responsibilities each day match our skills, personality, experience, and passions, incredible things can happen. That's especially true for Christians who see their work as an opportunity to honor God. As Solomon said, this kind of work leads to life!

Can work really be a source of God's blessing? Yes. If we find the right fit and we work to honor God, He unleashes His power in us and through us to accomplish great things and impact many people. At work, we can labor each day with integrity and enthusiasm because we know that what we do really counts. Fulfillment at work spills over to our time with our families. Instead of being angry or drained when we walk through the door at the end of the day, we can be excited about what God is doing, and our joy can spread to our spouses and children. In the community, we can be known as people who treat others fairly and who have earned respect. In all areas of life, we can sense God's purpose and presence and will delight in following Him.

How much does your work give life, and how much does it rob you of life?

What do you need to do to align your work with God's purposes and presence?

LIFE PROMISES

Because you are lukewarm, and neither cold nor hot, I will vomit you out of My mouth.

REVELATION 3:16

The fool folds his hands
     And consumes his own flesh.

ECCLESIASTES 4:5

Sow for yourselves righteousness;
     Reap in mercy.

HOSEA 10:12

THE CURSE OF MEDIOCRITY

SOME OF US HAVE LOST OUR PASSION for work, God, our families, and everything else in our lives. We drag ourselves in after a long day and collapse on the sofa only to tune out in front of the television. We no longer want to change the world. The most we can muster is changing the channel.

Even if the stress levels in our lives are only slightly above optimum, our minds, hearts, and bodies eventually wear down, and all forms of energy in our lives dissipate. We used to be excited about this goal or that purpose, but no longer. We used to care deeply about this person, but not anymore. All we want is to be left alone or to find somebody or something that will give us a few moments' pleasure. The curse of mediocrity ruins us and everyone we touch.

If your heart is lukewarm, step back, take stock of your stress level, notice any negative habits you've allowed to develop—and make changes. Don't settle for mediocrity any longer, but don't just add more activity to your life. To become fully alive again, you may have to eliminate even more than you add.

What activities, purposes, or people bring passion and purpose to your life?

To what extent has your life become mediocre? What do you need to do about it?

LIFE PROMISES

If you forgive men their trespasses, your heavenly Father will also forgive you.
MATTHEW 6:14

If [your brother] sins against you seven times in a day, and seven times in a day returns to you, saying, "I repent," you shall forgive him.
LUKE 17:4

Love prospers when a fault is forgiven,
but dwelling on it separates close
friends.
PROVERBS 17:9, NLT

LOVE GOD AND FORGIVE OTHERS

WE LIVE IN THE REAL WORLD, and we all get hurt by people from time to time. Sometimes, it's a small cut, but sometimes people leave us with gaping wounds. Anger is a normal response to injustice and hurt, but if anger isn't resolved, it soon turns into resentment and bitterness—which sour our attitudes and poison every relationship.

Bitterness is one of the chief causes of emotional stress and stress-related illnesses. We relive painful events over and over, and we rehearse ways we will get revenge. Our relationship with God becomes shallow and empty. Our lives are consumed with the hurt inflicted on us, but quite often, the person who hurt us isn't even aware of our daily emotional pain, and he or she might not even care.

The only remedy to break this pattern of bitterness is to forgive the one who hurt us. No, it won't be easy. The choice to forgive, though, opens the floodgates of God's presence and power. We just have to give up our bitterness first.

What are some consequences of bitterness in people's lives?

Is there someone you need to forgive? Start the process now.

LIFE PROMISES

If anyone among you thinks he is religious, and does not bridle his tongue but deceives his own heart, this one's religion is useless.
JAMES 1:26

Bear one another's burdens, and so fulfill the law of Christ.
GALATIANS 6:2

Confess your trespasses to one another, and pray for one another, that you may be healed.
JAMES 5:16

CONTENT OF THE HEART

OUR LANGUAGE AND TONE OF VOICE reflect the content of our hearts. If our hearts are in alignment with Christ's love and purposes, our tongues communicate warmth, forgiveness, acceptance, and wisdom. If our hearts aren't aligned with God's mission, however, we may claim to be following Christ but we are deceiving ourselves. Our speech, then, is an accurate measuring device that shows the true content of our hearts.

Religion promises to put us in touch with God, to enable us to experience His presence, and to change our lives. The inability to control our tongues shows that God hasn't actually touched our hearts, transformation hasn't taken place, and the grand promises haven't become true for us.

This sobering assessment may be painful, but it can be the beginning of a new day! The realization that our hearts are still hard can bring us to a point where we cry out for God to work deeply, powerfully, and specifically in our lives. A fearless and searching inventory of our tongues and our hearts may be heart wrenching, but not nearly as painful as finding out later that our religion has been useless.

What does your speech in the past twenty-four hours indicate about the content of your heart?

What changes need to be made so that your religion isn't useless?

LIFE PROMISES

Pursue peace with all people, and holiness, without which no one will see the Lord: looking carefully lest anyone fall short of the grace of God; lest any root of bitterness springing up cause trouble, and by this many become defiled.

HEBREWS 12:14-15

The heart knows its own bitterness,
    And a stranger does not share its joy.

PROVERBS 14:10

Let all bitterness, wrath, anger, clamor, and evil speaking be put away from you, with all malice.

EPHESIANS 4:31

ROOTS OF BITTERNESS

CERTAIN KINDS OF ROOTS can be dug up, dried, ground, and mixed with oil to make dyes to color fabric. And as any housewife could tell us, a dye misused causes a terrible stain. Bitterness is like a misused dye—it colors how we look at life, and it stains every relationship.

People who are bitter feel they have every right to their feelings and perspectives. They *feel like* victims because they *are* victims. God doesn't promise protection from every hurt we experience, but He doesn't want our anger and hurt to fester into bitterness and ruin every aspect of our lives.

Bitter people look for fights. They may say they don't like them, but they actually thrive on the adrenaline produced by intense disagreements. Instead, God wants us to stop this process before it starts: to pursue peace with all people. When they hurt us, we are to forgive them quickly. We need to watch out so that patterns of recrimination don't steal our joy, sap our energy, and ruin our ability to represent Christ.

Bitterness is serious business. It's a cancer that can't be tolerated, or it'll kill us. And it's contagious.

What does it mean to pursue peace with someone you disagree with?

How can you overcome bitterness?

LIFE PROMISES

The hand of the diligent will rule,
    But the lazy man will be put to
        forced labor.
PROVERBS 12:24

See . . . that you walk circumspectly,
not as fools but as wise, redeeming
the time, because the days are evil.
EPHESIANS 5:15-16

Because of laziness the building decays,
    And through idleness of hands the
        house leaks.
ECCLESIASTES 10:18

DELAYED DECISION

IF WE WANT TO DELAY making a decision, we can always find an excuse. And some of us are board-certified experts! After all, we don't want to decide now because

> the situation may change,
> the problem might completely go away,
> somebody may come up with a better solution, or
> we might win the lottery or a tornado might blow
>   us away—either way, we won't have to make
>   that decision!

Sometimes, we put up with an incredible mess because we're afraid of making a mistake. Certainly, we need to think through decisions so we choose the best option, but sooner or later, it's time to act. Procrastination is paralysis by fear, not astute planning. If you regularly have difficulty making decisions, look below the surface to identify your fears, and address them. No excuses!

What are some fears that can lead to procrastination?

How can I address my fears so that they no longer interfere with my life?

LIFE PROMISES

[Jesus said,] "The second . . . is this: 'You shall love your neighbor as yourself.' There is no other commandment greater than these."
MARK 12:31

Owe no one anything except to love one another, for he who loves another has fulfilled the law.
ROMANS 13:8

There is one Lawgiver, who is able to save and to destroy. Who are you to judge another?
JAMES 4:12

YOUR NEIGHBOR

JESUS SAYS THAT OUR LOVE for others should compare favorably to the attention we give to our own needs. When we're hungry, we find something in the refrigerator. When we're sleepy, we go to bed. We don't spend a lot of time wondering if we have this need or that one. If it's obvious, we just meet it. Our love for others should have the same reflexive quality: When we see their needs, we simply meet those needs.

Too often, we get wrapped up in our own little worlds, and we're consumed with our own needs without even noticing the needs of those around us. Or we're so exhausted at the end of each day that we can't imagine giving out to anyone else, such as to demanding kids or a spouse who is at least as tired as we are.

We have to break this cycle, back up, regroup, and bring some sanity to our lives so we'll have the perspective, energy, and compassion for the people we see each day, and especially those who live under the same roof with us. Then we can love them like we love ourselves.

Describe what it means to love someone the way you love yourself.

What are some practical things you can do to have more energy to devote to loving others?

LIFE PROMISES

Blessed is the man
> Who walks not in the counsel of
> the ungodly,
> Nor stands in the path of sinners,
> Nor sits in the seat of the scornful.

PSALM 1:1

No temptation has overtaken you except such as is common to man; but God is faithful, who will not allow you to be tempted beyond what you are able, but with the temptation will also make the way of escape, that you may be able to bear it.

1 CORINTHIANS 10:13

The highway of the upright is to depart
> from evil;
> He who keeps his way preserves
> his soul.

PROVERBS 16:17

A CROWNING ACHIEVEMENT

HOW DO WE ENDURE TEMPTATION? First, we have to recognize it. Far too often, we glamorize sin, excuse it, laugh at it, and let it become a normal part of our lives. White lies, sexual jokes, gossip, a critical attitude, and many other behaviors are part of life for most people—including many Christians. We won't resist the temptation to sin if we don't realize it's destructive.

When we recognize the temptation, we need to get as far away from it as possible. Nature, though, abhors a vacuum, so we need to replace the temptation with something good and wholesome and honoring to God and the people in our lives. Read inspiring books, listen to uplifting songs and talks, hang out with people who build others up instead of tearing them down, speak words of hope and affirmation.

Nobody said these things are easy. Resisting and enduring temptation take focused attention and energy, and they require tenacity to keep resisting when the temptation rises again out of nowhere. But James tells us that God generously rewards, with the crown of life, those who hang in there—what a reward!

What are the most common temptations you face each day?

What are some ways you can recognize them, resist them, replace them, and endure?

See James 1:12.

LIFE PROMISES

Cease listening to instruction, my son,
    And you will stray from the words
        of knowledge.
PROVERBS 19:27

My beloved brethren, let every man
be swift to hear, slow to speak, slow to
wrath; for the wrath of man does not
produce the righteousness of God.
JAMES 1:19-20

[Jesus said,] "To those who listen to
my teaching, more understanding
will be given, and they will have an
abundance of knowledge. But for those
who are not listening, even what little
understanding they have will be taken
away from them."
MATTHEW 13:12, NLT

LISTEN CAREFULLY

MANY STUDENTS drive their parents crazy by listening to music while they study. "Oh, it doesn't distract me at all," the kids claim. "It's just background noise. I really don't even hear it."

In the same way, we can tune out the Holy Spirit's whispers and become oblivious to His communication with us. The Spirit speaks "a word behind" us, gently nudging us in a direction and reminding us of a truth from God's Word. He never shouts, and He never demands. He always lets us make our own choices, even if those choices lead to pain and heartache.

For many of us, however, the whisper of the Spirit is drowned out by the noise of our culture. A hectic pace, demands at work and home, to-do lists, and the stress of living modern life create a buzz that makes it difficult to hear the Spirit. When we realize what we're missing, we make adjustments. We carve out time to be alone and to be quiet, to read and to reflect, and to stop everything so we can really listen. If we practice enough, listening becomes a way of life.

If you aren't listening enough to the Spirit, what are you missing?

What can you do today to carve out time to listen?

See Isaiah 30:21.

LIFE PROMISES

[Jesus said,] "What will it profit a man if he gains the whole world, and loses his own soul?"

MARK 8:36

You shall love the LORD your God with all your heart, with all your soul, and with all your strength.

DEUTERONOMY 6:5

I will be glad and rejoice in Your mercy,
    For You have considered my
        trouble;
    You have known my soul in
        adversities.

PSALM 31:7

THE ONE TRADE
YOU SHOULD NEVER MAKE

GOD HAS CREATED US to live in two worlds, and while the spiritual is most important, our culture tends to value the tangible. We devote our time to making more money, and we spend our money getting more and more stuff. Some of us use our wealth as chips to show that we're smarter and sharper than others. Some, though, don't really care what others have. We just want as much as we can get to make our lives as pleasant as possible.

Jesus made the stark, sobering observation that the value of a single soul is greater than all the gold, oil, real estate, jewels, stocks, cars, and everything else of value on the planet. Jesus died to rescue our souls from eternal death. He died for our family members, our neighbors, the cranky old guy down the street, and the natives in the middle of the Amazon basin.

One of our most important, and yet one of the most difficult, tasks is to shift our attention from what is visible to what is invisible, from the tangible to the eternal, from what will rust and rot to what will last forever.

What's the lure of "stuff"? Why do we let it rule (or at least shape) our lives?

How would your life be different if you were gripped with the reality that a single soul is more important than all the world's wealth?

LIFE PROMISES

Those who are wise shall shine
    Like the brightness of the
      firmament,
    And those who turn many to
      righteousness
    Like the stars forever and ever.
DANIEL 12:3

Happy is the man who finds wisdom,
    And the man who gains
      understanding.
PROVERBS 3:13

God gives wisdom and knowledge and
joy to a man who is good in His sight.
ECCLESIASTES 2:26

BEING A NORTH STAR

FOR CENTURIES, mariners used the North Star to determine their courses on the seas. Whenever they got lost, they could make course corrections based on that fixed point in the sky, and in clear weather conditions, it kept them on the right track night after night.

Wise people serve as signposts in the same way. Rigorous faith in a good, powerful, and all-knowing God makes them excellent examples to others in their families, at work, at church, and in their neighborhoods. Like a well-lit path or the unmistakable sentinel in the night sky, those whose lives are characterized by steadfast faith show others the way to live.

We don't become signposts and stars in a flash. We gain wisdom from the powerful combination of studying God's Word, being sensitive to God's Spirit, and spending time with people who are truly wise. These efforts require an investment of time, energy, and emotion. Is it worth it? For a while, it may not seem so. The early stages of spiritual discovery often bring more questions than answers, but if we are persistent, the pieces begin to come together.

Do you want to be the kind of wise person who has a profound influence on others? Why or why not?

Are you willing to pay the price? Explain your answer.

LIFE PROMISES

There are diversities of gifts, but the same Spirit.

1 CORINTHIANS 12:4

Having then gifts differing according to the grace that is given to us, let us use them: if prophecy, let us prophesy in proportion to our faith; or ministry, let us use it in our ministering; he who teaches, in teaching; he who exhorts, in exhortation; he who gives, with liberality; he who leads, with diligence; he who shows mercy, with cheerfulness.

ROMANS 12:6-8

If anyone speaks, let him speak as the oracles of God. If anyone ministers, let him do it as with the ability which God supplies, that in all things God may be glorified through Jesus Christ.

1 PETER 4:11

DISCOVER
YOUR STRENGTHS

GOD HAS GIVEN EACH OF US abilities that we can use to fulfill our God-given dreams. However, sometimes we get stuck focusing on the wrong things when we can't discern how to use these abilities. Don't focus on your weaknesses; focus on your strengths. When your work responsibilities fit your God-given abilities, you're in the jet stream of accomplishment. You're far more creative, more energetic, more relaxed, and more willing to help others who need a hand.

Some of us have been caught in dead-end jobs for years, and we've lost hope of ever finding something that fulfills us. Certainly, God can take us through valleys from time to time to teach us important lessons, but life need not be a perpetual valley. We cannot be passive. We need to take initiative to uncover our latent talents and use them with all our hearts. It's not optional. Someday, we will stand before God to give an account of our time here on earth. On that day, He will ask us how we used the talents He gave us. I want to hear Him say, "Well done!" Don't you?

What are the activities and responsibilities that rev your engine?

What do you need to do to refine your career so that your job fits your God-given talents?

Many sorrows shall be to the wicked;
But he who trusts in the LORD,
mercy shall surround him.
Be glad in the LORD and rejoice, you
righteous;
And shout for joy, all you upright
in heart!

PSALM 32:10-11

The LORD knows the way of the
righteous,
But the way of the ungodly shall
perish.

PSALM 1:6

"There is no peace," says the LORD, "for
the wicked."

ISAIAH 48:22

UPRIGHT OR UPTIGHT?

BAD DECISIONS, especially those that are caused by
our selfishness and that result in others' pain, create
tremendous stress. If we don't turn to God quickly, we
can multiply our "sorrows" with outbursts of anger
when others point out our faults, with lies as we try to
cover them up, and with ruined relationships because
people can't trust us.

God doesn't demand perfection from us—just
honest and thankful hearts. Thankfulness is one of
the chief characteristics of a person who walks with
God. We can be thankful for all manner of things:
our homes, our health, our families and friends, our
nation, and countless other blessings. But if we're
honest about the darkness in our hearts, perhaps one
blessing stands out above the rest: the infinite mercy
of God.

We can't attain "upright hearts" by self-effort. Having
a clean and pure heart comes only from the kindness of
God to look at the worst of our sins and choose to forgive us. It's enough to make us shout for joy!

*What are some selfish choices in your life that have
made you uptight?*

*Take those to God and thank Him for His wonderful
mercy and forgiveness.*

LIFE PROMISES

May the Lord direct your hearts into the love of God and into the patience of Christ.

2 THESSALONIANS 3:5

Let us not grow weary while doing good, for in due season we shall reap if we do not lose heart.

GALATIANS 6:9

It is God who works in you both to will and to do for His good pleasure.

PHILIPPIANS 2:13

COURAGEOUS CONVERSATIONS

MOST OF US SPEND OUR LIVES trying to project an image of beauty and competence. Nehemiah had a plum job. He was working closely with the king, and he lived a life of luxury. His heart, though, beat in unison with God's heart. He cared about the things God cares about, and when he heard that the people in Jerusalem were suffering, his heart broke. He didn't minimize the problem, and he didn't fly into a panic of mindless activity. Instead, he let the brutal truth sink in, and he responded appropriately: He sat down and wept.

Nehemiah had a courageous conversation with the messenger, then he had a courageous conversation with God. Only courageous people are known for their honesty. It's a lot easier to look the other way when we see needs in our lives or in the lives of people around us. We can give the excuse that we've tried as hard as we can or that we don't have time to help a person in need. But excuses don't cut it. Like Nehemiah, we need to let the truth sink into our hearts so we can respond with genuine compassion.

What are some needs in your own life and in the lives of those around you?

How would being honest about those needs become a springboard for change?

See Nehemiah 1.

Delight yourself also in the LORD,
    And He shall give you the desires
        of your heart.
Commit your way to the LORD,
    Trust also in Him,
    And He shall bring it to pass.
PSALM 37:4-5

My son, give me your heart,
    And let your eyes observe my ways.
PROVERBS 23:26

Be kindly affectionate to one another
with brotherly love, in honor giving
preference to one another.
ROMANS 12:10

DELIGHT = DESIRES

THE SOURCE OF OUR DELIGHT shapes the nature of our desires. If we delight in someone, we genuinely want that person to be happy. If we delight in acquiring bigger and better possessions, we won't be able to stop until we have enough to satisfy us—which never happens. And if we delight in God, our interactions with Him shape our hearts so that we gradually desire what He desires and value what He values.

To delight in God is to be satisfied and, in fact, thrilled with His love, forgiveness, and purpose for us. As we know and love Him more, we want to pursue His will, we make choices to follow His leading, and we take action to accomplish things He has directed us to do.

It doesn't take a psychologist to unlock the secrets of our desires. We need only to look at what excites us, what frustrates us, and what hopes and fears fill our minds. We can choose, though, to focus on God, to delight in Him so that He gradually changes the desires of our hearts to fit more with His.

What do your joys, frustrations, hopes, and fears say about your desires?

To what degree would you say you genuinely delight in God?

LIFE PROMISES

Greater love has no one than this, than
to lay down one's life for his friends.
JOHN 15:13

God so loved the world that He gave
His only begotten Son, that whoever
believes in Him should not perish
but have everlasting life.
JOHN 3:16

The secret of the LORD is with those
       who fear Him,
   And He will show them His
       covenant.
PSALM 25:14

ULTIMATE MODEL

IT'S EASY TO TALK A GOOD GAME. We say we're committed to our spouses, our kids, and our friends, but the measure of love is the depth of sacrifice we are willing to make for them. How often are we willing to forgo our own pleasures, comforts, and desires for the good of another person?

We see genuine love in times of crisis, when a person risks life and peace to help someone in need. Caring for a chronically sick relative is a demonstration of authentic, "greater love," as are being patient with an annoying person, forgiving a habitual offender, and speaking truth when it would be easier to run away and hide.

We live in a self-absorbed world where personal rights reign supreme, but every society has been selfish to one degree or another. Self-sacrifice is as rare as it is powerful; however, it's the inherent nature of believers who follow the example of the One who risked all and gave all for those who didn't understand or appreciate what He was doing. His life and His death are the ultimate models of love.

What does authentic love look like to you?

In what ways was Christ's life as much of a sacrifice as His death?

LIFE PROMISES

See . . . that you walk circumspectly,
not as fools but as wise, redeeming
the time, because the days are evil.
EPHESIANS 5:15-16

We urge you, brethren, that you
increase more and more; that you
also aspire to lead a quiet life, to mind
your own business, and to work with
your own hands, as we commanded
you, that you may walk properly
toward those who are outside, and
that you may lack nothing.
1 THESSALONIANS 4:10-12

Be steadfast, immovable, always
abounding in the work of the Lord,
knowing that your labor is not in vain
in the Lord.
1 CORINTHIANS 15:58

KEEPING TRACK OF TIME

PEOPLE WASTE TIME in two very different ways. We usually associate the term with people who procrastinate and don't do the things they're responsible for. But another, more insidious form is probably more common, yet not as obvious: investing time and energy in the wrong pursuits. We waste time by worrying too much about what others think of us, reliving past conversations because we're afraid we said the wrong thing, or projecting our fears into the future. And we waste time when we measure our lives by the fullness of our schedules instead of the richness of our relationships.

Paul reminds us that every minute counts. We are in a cosmic but invisible struggle between the forces of good and evil. Time is one of our greatest resources in this fight. It allows us to connect with our Commander and to carry out His directions. Far too often, though, we don't think of time this way.

The goal isn't to be busy. We redeem the time by seeing every moment as a gift from God to be used to honor Him.

What are the most common ways you see people wasting time?

How would it change your life to realize that every moment is a gift from God to be redeemed and used to honor Him?

LIFE PROMISES

We are His workmanship, created in
Christ Jesus for good works, which God
prepared beforehand that we should
walk in them.
EPHESIANS 2:10

[David said,] "I will praise You, for I am
        fearfully and wonderfully made;
    Marvelous are Your works,
    And that my soul knows very well."
PSALM 139:14

There are diversities of activities, but it
is the same God who works all in all.
1 CORINTHIANS 12:6

CRAFTED

OUR ABILITIES, personalities, and physical features are no accident. God has crafted each of us just the way He wanted to. Paul wrote that we are God's "workmanship." We are created by God to do good works and bring glory to His Kingdom.

God crafts each of us by using His skill to shape our personalities and give us the abilities and appearances He has chosen for us. No one is created just like another because no one has the same purpose God has given each of us. Paul also tells his readers that God's purpose isn't something He dreams up along the way. God prepared His purpose for us long ago, "before the foundation of the world."

When we feel prideful because we've accomplished a lot, we need to realize where our abilities came from. On the other hand, if we're confused or discouraged because we can't seem to discover the meaning for our lives, we can rest assured that Almighty God has a divine purpose for us.

How do you respond to the fact that you are God's workmanship?

What are some ways God has used you to accomplish "good works"?

See Ephesians 1:4.

Let them shout for joy and be glad,
    Who favor my righteous cause;
    And let them say continually,
    "Let the Lord be magnified,
    Who has pleasure in the
        prosperity of His servant."
PSALM 35:27

These are Your servants and Your
people, whom You have redeemed by
Your great power, and by Your strong
hand.
NEHEMIAH 1:10

You shall walk in all the ways which
the Lord your God has commanded
you, that you may live and that it may
be well with you, and that you may
prolong your days.
DEUTERONOMY 5:33

A CAUSE WORTH DYING FOR

IN OUR CULTURE, many self-absorbed people focus their energies on doing the newest activity that promises the most pleasure and on getting the latest technology that's supposed to make life easier. But those things don't satisfy for very long. God made us so that our hearts long for a transcendent purpose. We want to live for something much bigger than ourselves.

Causes come in every stripe and color. Some people get energized for a political candidate who promises to change a city, state, or nation. Others devote themselves to preserving the planet or helping the homeless. In war, soldiers fight and die for the freedom of those back home.

Many causes are noble, but most of them have only temporary results. Beyond even those noble intentions and actions, however, the cause for every believer is to know Christ and to honor Him in everything we do. While the cause of Christ involves reaching the lost and changing lives, ultimately the goal is to please the One who gave His life for us. That's the cause that makes us shout for joy!

What are some causes your friends are excited about?

If an objective observer looked at your life, what would he or she conclude that you are devoted to? Explain your answer.

LIFE PROMISES

Let us not grow weary while doing good, for in due season we shall reap if we do not lose heart. Therefore, as we have opportunity, let us do good to all, especially to those who are of the household of faith.

GALATIANS 6:9-10

Do not be overcome by evil, but overcome evil with good.

ROMANS 12:21

Who is wise and understanding among you? Let him show by good conduct that his works are done in the meekness of wisdom.

JAMES 3:13

BEING RIGHT
BY DOING GOOD

WE SOMETIMES HEAR SOMEONE cynically say, "No good deed goes unpunished." Occasionally, there's a measure of truth in the statement. When we try to do the right thing, it can backfire and get people upset with us. But our good deeds never backfire with God. We have the promise that He always rewards us for doing the right thing when we help others.

"Doing good" is an exceptionally broad category. We do good when we notice something positive in a person's life and affirm it, when we take time to listen, when we love someone enough to speak the truth and confront him or her about a sin, when we set aside our agenda to offer a helping hand, and in countless other ways. Paul said we should do these things "as we have opportunity," which is all day every day!

The world is watching to see if we really love one another. If they see that we genuinely support one another with actions, not just lip service, they may become convinced that faith in Christ makes a difference.

Who are some people you know who are examples of those who do good?

What are some things you can do today for others?

LIFE PROMISES

You shall not bear false witness against your neighbor.
EXODUS 20:16

Keep your tongue from evil,
And your lips from speaking deceit.
PSALM 34:13

Do not lie to one another, since you have put off the old man with his deeds.
COLOSSIANS 3:9

TELL THE TRUTH

THE COMMAND to avoid bearing false witness sounds like a script from a John Grisham novel. It certainly means to speak "the whole truth and nothing but the truth" under oath in court, but God wants us to be honest both in and out of the courtroom.

We break this commandment when we exaggerate the truth to impress our friends or coworkers, and we break it when we gossip and ruin others' reputations. And quite often, the devious thrill of gossiping pushes us over the edge so that we make sure we amplify any perceived wrong the person has done.

There are many reasons to tell the truth and to tell it with humility and grace. When we are committed to the truth, we don't have to look over our shoulders all the time to see whether we're going to get caught. The truth may be painful at times, but it shows that we trust God with reality instead of trying to create our own version of it. And eventually we will have to face the consequences of our deceptions. These are good reasons to speak the truth all the time.

What are some benefits and consequences of "white" lies?

How can you take steps to speak the truth instead of exaggerating or deceiving?

LIFE PROMISES

We must all appear before the judgment seat of Christ, that each one may receive the things done in the body, according to what he has done, whether good or bad.
2 CORINTHIANS 5:10

You shall do what is right and good in the sight of the LORD, that it may be well with you.
DEUTERONOMY 6:18

The world is passing away, and the lust of it; but he who does the will of God abides forever.
1 JOHN 2:17

PERFORMANCE REVIEW

WHEN YOU KNOW you're going to meet with your boss in a couple of weeks for a performance review, how do you act? We do whatever it takes so that the review is as positive as possible. In other words, the reality of the review makes a difference in our choices.

The Bible tells us that we'll be called into the Boss's office one day for the ultimate performance review. We'll stand before Jesus Christ to give an account of our choices as Christians. On that day, you and I will look Jesus in the eye as He reviews the times we made selfish choices and the times we were gracious to others, the moments we hoped no one was watching and the ones we hoped the world knew what we were doing. All our selfishness will burn up and vanish, and we'll be left with the reward we've earned by pleasing God.

And this is the only performance review by Christ we'll ever experience. For that reason, we need to get ready now by aligning our lives with God's purposes and His ways. I want that review to be a good experience for me. How about you?

If Jesus' review of your life happened today, what would He be pleased with, and what would He be unhappy about?

How does the future reality of this review change how you will act today?

LIFE PROMISES

You shall keep My Sabbaths and
reverence My sanctuary: I am the
LORD.

LEVITICUS 19:30

Rest in the LORD, and wait patiently
        for Him.

PSALM 37:7

O LORD, be gracious to us;
        We have waited for You.
        Be [our] arm every morning,
        Our salvation also in the time
            of trouble.

ISAIAH 33:2

REAL REST

MANY OF US don't know how to rest. We're geared up 24/7 to accomplish as much as we possibly can while at work and to play hard in the evenings and on weekends. We experience what some call "hurry sickness," rushing around so much that we make ourselves (and others) physically and emotionally sick. Some of us wear stress as a badge of honor. We take pride in our packed schedules, but we don't realize the damage we're inflicting on ourselves. One man had a revelation: "My pride about always being busy was sick. Being in a hurry all the time generated a tremendous amount of anger, and I never gave myself time to decompress."

The Sabbath, however, isn't just a day off for us to do nothing. It should be filled with things that refresh us: taking time to worship God; investing in our family relationships; reading a good book; enjoying a hobby; and yes, kicking off our shoes and relaxing. A lifestyle of being always on the go is addictive, and any addiction is hard to overcome. It takes focused attention, discipline, courage, and the encouragement of others who are on the same path.

Do you see any "hurry sickness" in your life?

What are some specific things you can do to make a Sabbath rest meaningful?

LIFE PROMISES

"Be angry, and do not sin": do not let
the sun go down on your wrath, nor
give place to the devil.
EPHESIANS 4:26-27

The discretion of a man makes him
    slow to anger,
    And his glory is to overlook a
    transgression.
PROVERBS 19:11

The Lord is merciful and gracious,
    Slow to anger, and abounding in
    mercy.
PSALM 103:8

HEALTHY COMMUNICATION

ONE OF THE MOST IMPORTANT LESSONS any of us can learn is to control our responses to difficult people and stressful situations. All of us remember when we said too much, too intensely, and too often.

When we face someone who is defiant or annoying, our natural response is to try to control. We may try to intimidate, we may run away, or we may appease the person to get the conflict over as quickly as possible. Those tactics work just fine—for a moment—but they don't create positive, healthy habits of communication.

In these situations, we often interrupt to say what we believe needs to be said. We fail to ask for the other person's point of view because, to be honest, we don't want to hear it! It takes only a few seconds for our anger to erupt, and then, all that's left is picking up the pieces after the relationship is shattered. We need to recognize the damage inflicted by our current responses to others, and then, with a fresh wave of motivation, take steps to change. You can do it. It just takes practice.

How would this strategy have changed your last difficult conversation?

Imagine using it in that conversation. Imagine using it in the next one.

LIFE PROMISES

God created man in His own image; in
the image of God He created him; male
and female He created them.
GENESIS 1:27

You formed my inward parts;
>   You covered me in my mother's
>   womb.
I will praise You, for I am fearfully and
>   wonderfully made.
PSALM 139:13-14

By Him all things were created that are
in heaven and that are on earth, visible
and invisible, whether thrones or
dominions or principalities or powers.
All things were created through Him
and for Him.
COLOSSIANS 1:16

DESIGNER LABEL

WHEN WE WERE GROWING UP, we got our sense of identity by receiving messages from our parents and later from our friends, teachers, and employers. But the most powerful message about who we are comes from God, who crafted us with skill and love. No matter what anyone else says about us, we aren't accidents of nature, and we aren't mistakes. Almighty God has made us, and He has imprinted His image on us. To be sure, sin has tarnished that image, but we still possess a portion of the dignity God originally intended.

When you look in the mirror, what do you see? Do you see someone who was created by God, who is a person of infinite worth? If we see ourselves that way, we instantly realize two things: We desperately need the grace of God to forgive us when we fail to live up to our identity, and we need to conform our lives to fit our status as the King's kids. We should stop monkeying around and begin to act like the children of the King so we will be a reflection of all He desires us to be!

When you look in the mirror, what do you see?

How would it affect your attitude and choices today if you saw yourself as someone who has been skillfully crafted by God?

Blessed is he who considers the poor;
>   The LORD will deliver him in time of
>   trouble.

PSALM 41:1

Let each one give as he purposes in his
heart, not grudgingly or of necessity;
for God loves a cheerful giver. And
God is able to make all grace abound
toward you, that you, always having all
sufficiency in all things, may have an
abundance for every good work.

2 CORINTHIANS 9:7-8

He who has pity on the poor lends to
>   the LORD,
>   And He will pay back what he has
>   given.

PROVERBS 19:17

WHAT GOES AROUND COMES AROUND

IT'S TECHNICALLY CALLED "THE LAW OF THE HARVEST," but we commonly say "What goes around comes around" to refer to the law of reaping what we sow. We see the effects of this "law" every day. When we're angry and snap at people, they often snap back at us. When we help someone, the one we helped sometimes comes to our rescue when we are in need.

When we give to someone who is poor, that person can't pay us back, but blessings seem to come our way from out of the blue. It's God. He's the One who sees what we've done and takes care of us in return. That's like Him. Jesus said that it's no big deal to give to those who can give back to us. The really big deal is to give to those who can't repay us.

Who are the poor around us? They are real people with real needs and real hopes and dreams. God wants us to consider them, to imagine what their lives are like so that we learn to genuinely care. When we care, we'll find a way to take action.

Consider the poor. Who are they? What are their lives like?

What is one thing you can do to care for one of them?

LIFE PROMISES

Let your "Yes" be "Yes," and your "No,"
"No." For whatever is more than these
is from the evil one.
MATTHEW 5:37

Show me Your ways, O LORD;
    Teach me Your paths.
PSALM 25:4

Reject profane and old wives' fables,
and exercise yourself toward godliness.
For bodily exercise profits a little, but
godliness is profitable for all things,
having promise of the life that now is
and of that which is to come.
1 TIMOTHY 4:7-8

THE DANGER OF SITUATIONAL ETHICS

WE WANT TO SUCCEED and get ahead—there's nothing wrong with that, unless we take unethical shortcuts. In business and in all other relationships, we're tempted to tell people what they want to hear so that the deal will close, we'll get the promotion, our spouses will appreciate us, our kids will behave, and our friends will be more impressed with us. But telling people what they want to hear is, at its heart, manipulation, not integrity.

One of the marks of a person who is vitally connected to Christ is the courage to speak the truth— with clarity and grace. However, we're only human. When we're tempted to exaggerate to impress or withhold information to protect ourselves, we need to fight against it and say, "This is the truth. This is what happened."

Yes, we can certainly complain that "everybody shades the truth" from time to time, but that doesn't matter to Jesus. Every time we're tempted to manipulate people's responses by shading the truth, we have a choice: to follow the evil one or follow Christ.

What are some common situations in which you are tempted to shade the truth to manipulate people's responses to you?

What would it do for your self-esteem and your walk with God to choose the simple truth?

A wrathful man stirs up strife,
But he who is slow to anger allays
contention.
PROVERBS 15:18

Cease from anger, and forsake wrath;
Do not fret—it only causes harm.
PSALM 37:8

Keep the unity of the Spirit in the bond
of peace.
EPHESIANS 4:3

RUDE LEADS TO RUDE

THE PACE AND PRESSURES of life have escalated in recent years. Only two generations ago, most Americans lived on farms, where the pace was measured in seasons. A generation ago, many people still walked to work, and they enjoyed a stable family life, nightly dinners together, and minimal distractions. Today, greater mobility and high expectations create tremendous stress, and when stressed people don't get what they demand, the lid blows off!

We call them hotheads because the slightest provocation causes steam to blow out of their ears and produces fiery words. The people around them are just as stressed, so in reaction, they erupt like volcanoes! Cooler heads, though, can reduce the fire and tension.

God calls us to be peacemakers. To be peacemakers, we first have to be at peace with God and not be stressed out ourselves. Our first task, then, is to take stock of the stresses in our lives and take steps to reduce them. Only then can we be slow to anger and reduce the fires of anger in people around us.

When have you seen tension escalate between angry people?

Are you a peacemaker? If not, what can you do to reduce stress so you can have a cool head?

LIFE PROMISES

Whatever you do, do it heartily, as to the Lord and not to men, knowing that from the Lord you will receive the reward of the inheritance; for you serve the Lord Christ.

COLOSSIANS 3:23-24

Be strong and do not let your hands be weak, for your work shall be rewarded!

2 CHRONICLES 15:7

God is not unjust to forget your work and labor of love which you have shown toward His name, in that you have ministered to the saints, and do minister.

HEBREWS 6:10

TURNING A CAREER INTO A CALLING

WHY DO WE GO TO WORK each day? Most of us get out of bed and head to work for a number of good reasons: to provide for our families, to enjoy interaction, creativity, and success. But when we face the inevitable difficulties of an unreasonable boss, a downturn in the economy, a heavy workload, or genuine failure, where can we find our motivation?

In his letter to the Colossians, Paul gives instructions to husbands, wives, fathers, and children. Then he turns his attention to another segment of society: slaves. They are asked to do the most but are given the least praise. Paul encourages them to do their menial work "heartily," with real enthusiasm as they remember that they are working first for God Himself, not their human masters. But Paul also assures them that God will eventually reward their honest work.

We can get out of bed each day with the assurance that we are working for the Lord and that our good attitude and hard work will be richly rewarded—if not now, they will be someday by the God of the universe. That perspective changes our motivation and attitude at work!

What difference would it make for you to realize that you are working primarily for Christ, not for your boss or your company?

What needs to happen in your thoughts, attitudes, and actions to reflect this perspective?

LIFE PROMISES

We also glory in tribulations, knowing that tribulation produces perseverance; and perseverance, character; and character, hope. Now hope does not disappoint, because the love of God has been poured out in our hearts by the Holy Spirit who was given to us.
ROMANS 5:3-5

[The Lord says,] "I will give you a new heart and put a new spirit within you; I will take the heart of stone out of your flesh and give you a heart of flesh."
EZEKIEL 36:26

The Lord is good,
> A stronghold in the day of trouble;
> And He knows those who trust
>> in Him.

NAHUM 1:7

PRISON OR CLASSROOM

LIFE IS ALL ABOUT PERSPECTIVE. If we see difficult people and painful situations as threats, they become prisons for our souls. Like inmates in medieval dungeons, we languish away for days and weeks, wishing the problems would just go away, or we try frantically to get out any way we can.

Whether our problems are caused by our own mistakes, the sins of others, natural disasters, or anything else, our difficulties can, instead of dungeons, become classrooms where we learn life's greatest lessons.

In some circles today, Christian leaders teach that God wants everybody to have peace and plenty, lots of money, and all the happiness in the world. That may sell books, but it doesn't help much when God allows difficulties to take us deeper into a relationship of trusting Him. Paul recommends a different perspective, one that sees problems not as prisons but as classrooms where God gets our attention, transforms our character, and gives us strong hope in the things that are most valuable—His will and His ways. Eventually, the lessons take us to the heart of God, where we experience His kindness and love more deeply than ever before.

What are some difficulties in your life right now?

How would it change your response to them if you could see them as God's classroom?

LIFE PROMISES

[Paul said,] "I say . . . to everyone who is among you, not to think of himself more highly than he ought to think, but to think soberly, as God has dealt to each one a measure of faith."
ROMANS 12:3

[Jesus said,] "Peace I leave with you, My peace I give to you; not as the world gives do I give to you. Let not your heart be troubled, neither let it be afraid."
JOHN 14:27

May the God of hope fill you with all joy and peace in believing, that you may abound in hope by the power of the Holy Spirit.
ROMANS 15:13

THE CURE FOR CONCEIT

PEOPLE HAVE AN AMAZING CAPACITY for self-deception—either thinking too highly of themselves or too lowly. Both bring a lot of trouble. Inflated egos lead to boorish behavior, hurt relationships, and using people instead of loving them. Crushed egos cause people to build walls around their hearts and drive them to prove that they aren't that bad after all.

To correct mistaken self-perceptions, Paul instructs us to "think soberly," that is, to have God's perspective of ourselves. Each of us contains the image of God, but that image is tarnished by sin. One writer said we are equal parts saint and beast, which explains the inner conflict we experience.

By faith, we realize that God created us the way He wanted to, and we accept our abilities and talents as gifts from Him. Sin, though, clouds our hearts and distorts our thinking. We desperately need God's grace to restore us, and we need His wisdom to lead us. We are wonderfully created, tragically fallen, deeply loved, and completely forgiven. That's a sober assessment of each of us who call Christ our Savior and Friend.

What does it mean for you to think soberly, honestly, and truthfully about yourself?

How does the statement "We are wonderfully created, tragically fallen, deeply loved, and completely forgiven" give you a grasp on your self-worth?

LIFE PROMISES

Every prudent man acts with knowledge,
    But a fool lays open his folly.
PROVERBS 13:16

I will cry out to God Most High,
    To God who performs all things
        for me.
PSALM 57:2

We speak as messengers approved by
God to be entrusted with the Good
News. Our purpose is to please God,
not people. He alone examines the
motives of our hearts.
1 THESSALONIANS 2:4, NLT

COURSE CORRECTION

WHEN WE'RE YOUNG, we plan to take the world by storm. When we're in our middle years, we wonder how we got where we are. When we're older, we plan to leave a legacy. Many of us spend our lives making great and glorious plans, but only a few focus on what's really important.

One of the marks of maturity at any age is the ability to see through the urgent to discern what's significant. In our younger years, it seems that everything is urgent. We rush from one goal to another, seldom enjoying life along the way. Sooner or later, we learn that we shouldn't trust ourselves or some of our friends. We need a higher authority, and we turn to God for direction. Money, prestige, power, and possessions are measuring sticks of our culture, but God shakes His head at our compulsive pursuit of these things. They aren't wrong; they just aren't central.

If we discover God's purposes and pursue them with our whole hearts, our plans will follow His leading. And in the end, our plans—and the positive impact of a life lived for Him—will stand.

What are some things most people today think are really important?

What does God say is really important? How do your pursuits match up with God's purposes?

LIFE PROMISES

[Paul said,] "Meditate on [my teachings]; give yourself entirely to them, that your progress may be evident to all."
1 TIMOTHY 4:15

Seek first the kingdom of God and His righteousness, and all these things shall be added to you.
MATTHEW 6:33

Set your mind on things above, not on things on the earth.
COLOSSIANS 3:2

MODELING
THE RIGHT STUFF

WHEN PEOPLE FOLLOW US, what are they looking for?
Some want a parent figure, some want a big brother
or sister, and some want specific help in developing
a new business plan. Most followers, though, want to
follow leaders who know where they're going and have
genuine passion about getting there. Those two traits
aren't that complicated, but the combination is sur-
prisingly rare.

In his letter, Paul had given Timothy a list of instructions and the rationale to implement a strategy of
leadership. He gave him sound advice: Think long and
hard about all that I've written to you so that it sinks
deep below the surface and becomes an integral part of
your life. And that's not all. Don't just think about these
things; pour your life into them, everything you've got—
body, mind, and soul! When people see that, they'll sit
up and notice, and then they'll follow you.

Paul understood that leadership comes from the
heart. We may move bodies by our directions in staff
meetings, but we move hearts only when people are
convinced that we really understand what we're talk-
ing about and only when we show them that we are
devoted to the mission.

*Describe the level of your understanding of your role and
cause and your passion to accomplish your purpose.*

*What would "modeling the right stuff" look like in
your life?*

LIFE PROMISES

He who walks with integrity walks
        securely,
    But he who perverts his ways will
        become known.
PROVERBS 10:9

Let patience have its perfect work,
that you may be perfect and complete,
lacking nothing.
JAMES 1:4

Honest weights and scales are the
        LORD's;
    All the weights in the bag are
        His work.
PROVERBS 16:11

WALK WITH INTEGRITY

INTEGRITY HAS BEEN DESCRIBED as "doing the right thing even when nobody is looking." When we try to hide our sinful behavior behind a mask of lies, we live with the constant fear of somebody finding out. All of us know this experience to some degree. Some of us stay on track most of the time and only occasionally have to fear being found out, but others have lied so much to cover their tracks that they don't remember what's true anymore.

A clear conscience is a treasure, but it doesn't just happen. We can experience the peace of a clean heart and an uncluttered mind only if we make a rigorous commitment to live our lives in the presence of God and, when we fail, make things right quickly. There's nothing quite as chilling as knowing that you're being watched. When we live with the confidence that everything we do passes under the eyes of God, we will make sure we don't stray off track.

Everything we do is already known to God. It's a much wiser course to walk with integrity now.

What happens to you and your relationships when you try to wear a mask to hide your sin?

What would it (or does it) take for you to live with a clear conscience?

LIFE PROMISES

Not that I [Paul] speak in regard to need, for I have learned in whatever state I am, to be content: I know how to be abased, and I know how to abound. Everywhere and in all things I have learned both to be full and to be hungry, both to abound and to suffer need.

PHILIPPIANS 4:11-12

His divine power has given to us all things that pertain to life and godliness, through the knowledge of Him who called us by glory and virtue.

2 PETER 1:3

Do not let your heart envy sinners,
But be zealous for the fear of
the Lord all the day;
For surely there is a hereafter,
And your hope will not be cut off.

PROVERBS 23:17-18

THE ART OF CONTENTMENT

MANY OF US HAVE SOME MIXED-UP IDEAS about contentment. We think that if we can ever have this or that good thing, our lives will be better. If we thought about it more than a nanosecond, though, we'd realize that we know plenty of people who have this or who have successfully avoided that but still aren't any happier than we are.

We experience true contentment when external things lose their grip on our hearts and don't matter much anymore. Some of us get bent out of shape when we realize our favorite shirt is still at the cleaners. Paul's well of contentment was so deep that he could enjoy life with or without the most basic needs. He was content being full or going hungry, having many possessions or little to speak of, living a life of ease or suffering at the hands of evil men.

A poster in a college professor's office reads, "Happiness isn't having what you want; it's wanting what you have." Jealousy, envy, and greed suck any sense of contentment out of us. Replace those joy killers with gratitude for what you have, and listen to your heart sing!

What does this statement mean to you: "Happiness isn't having what you want; it's wanting what you have"?

What are some steps you need to take to learn the secret of contentment?

LIFE PROMISES

[Jesus said,] "Come to Me, all you who labor and are heavy laden, and I will give you rest."
MATTHEW 11:28

You would be secure, because there
        is hope;
    Yes, you would dig around you,
        and take your rest in safety.
JOB 11:18

It is vain for you to rise up early,
    To sit up late,
    To eat the bread of sorrows;
    For so He gives His beloved sleep.
PSALM 127:2

WHEN YOU ARE SO TIRED

IN A RECENT POLL, a large segment of Americans were asked the simple question, "How are you doing?" The number one answer given by thousands of respondents was simply, "Tired."

We've been had. Years ago, technology promised to make us more efficient so we could have more leisure time and more time with our families, but it hasn't worked out that way. Amazing advances in technology have made us far more efficient and productive, but our thirst for more has caused us to cram our schedules full of additional activities. Many families are so busy that they don't even have one dinner together each week!

The solution, we've tried to tell ourselves, is better time management or the latest technology, but that hasn't worked either. No, we need something radically different—a new focus with new priorities. Jesus invites us to come to Him. He doesn't promise to give us twenty-five-hour days or magically enable us to get everything checked off our lists each day. Instead, He invites us to trust Him and rest, to enjoy His love and let Him lead us so that we distinguish the *genuinely important* from the *seemingly urgent*.

What (if any) are some evidences in your life of chronic tiredness?

What would it look like for you to respond to Jesus' invitation?

The words of the LORD are pure words,
    Like silver tried in a furnace of earth,
    Purified seven times.

PSALM 12:6

Blessed are the pure in heart,
    For they shall see God.

MATTHEW 5:8

The fear of the LORD is clean, enduring
        forever;
    The judgments of the LORD are true
        and righteous altogether.

PSALM 19:9

PURE AND POWERFUL

WITH ALL THE TECHNOLOGY surrounding us, we hear thousands of messages every day. We are constantly distracted by e-mail, instant messaging, cell phones, and other devices. Linda Stone, formerly of Apple and Microsoft, observes, "We want to connect and be connected. We want to effectively scan for opportunity and optimize for the best opportunities, activities, and contacts, in any given moment."

Too often, we value all received messages equally. God's Word, though, is more precious and valuable than any other message sent to us. God's Word is absolutely perfect and in alignment with the character of God. It is the supreme measure of truth, and it imparts light and life to those who treasure it.

When we read and hear God's Word, we need to sit up and take notice. If we don't understand it, we need to dig deeper until we find out what it means. And when God uses His Word to redirect our steps, we are wise to say, "Yes, Lord. I'm listening." God's Word directs us along God's path, and that way is perfect for us each day.

How do you treat letters or e-mails that are especially meaningful to you?

What would it mean for you to truly treasure God's Word?

A word fitly spoken is like apples of gold
    In settings of silver.
PROVERBS 25:11

Should he reason with unprofitable talk,
    Or by speeches with which he can
        do no good?
JOB 15:3

The lips of the righteous feed many,
    But fools die for lack of wisdom.
PROVERBS 10:21

THE RIGHT WORD
AT THE RIGHT TIME

THE WISEST AND MOST EFFECTIVE PEOPLE are those who capture a moment by saying the right thing in the right way. Quite often, their statements seem to come from out of the blue because the tone of voice and the actual words speak a very different message from what most people expect. Instead of returning anger for anger and backing people into a corner, they calmly speak truth and give options. Instead of using a person's fears to control him or her, they soothe fear by speaking words of hope.

Researchers tell us that communication is largely nonverbal. Facial expressions, gestures, and the tone of voice relay our message most frequently. Words can be "fitly spoken" only if we say them with authenticity, really meaning what we say, and letting our faces, hands, and tone of voice carry the message too.

Messages have incredible power. They can build or destroy, instill hope or take it away. Think about the people you will see today. Some of them are hurting, some are angry, and some have lost hope. What would it mean for you to communicate powerful, life-giving messages of faith, hope, and love to those dear people?

Who are the people who have most often and most powerfully affirmed you and given you hope when you felt hopeless?

What are some messages you can give to particular people today?

LIFE PROMISES

It is better to hear the rebuke of the wise
    Than for a man to hear the song
        of fools.
ECCLESIASTES 7:5

If you listen to constructive criticism,
    you will be at home among the wise.
PROVERBS 15:31, NLT

Let the words of my mouth and the
        meditation of my heart
    Be acceptable in Your sight,
    O Lord, my strength and my
        Redeemer.
PSALM 19:14

FOOLISH SONGS

"I DIDN'T ENJOY HEARING IT, but I really needed to hear what you told me. Thank you." This was the response of a man whose boss had told him he wasn't getting a promotion. His boss explained the reasons the man had been bypassed, and instead of reacting defensively, he listened, accepted the truth, and made changes in his life.

One of the chief marks of maturity is the ability to hear correction. Far too often, we pursue relationships with people who tell us only what they think we want to hear. They tell us that we're brilliant, gifted, and right, and if anybody tries to correct us, our "friends" take our side and tell us we're victims of injustice.

Nobody likes to hear correction, but think of it this way: When we're sick, we take medicine to make us well. Only a fool would insist he doesn't need it! In the same way, when our hearts are sick, we need the medicine of truth from a wise "physician of the soul" who speaks truth to us. If we listen, we take steps on the path of health and hope.

How do you normally respond to correction?

How is correction from a wise person like medicine?

LIFE PROMISES

Whatever you want men to do to you,
do also to them, for this is the Law and
the Prophets.
MATTHEW 7:12

Let not mercy and truth forsake you;
    Bind them around your neck,
    Write them on the tablet of
        your heart.
PROVERBS 3:3

[Jesus said,] "'Honor your father and
your mother,' and, 'You shall love your
neighbor as yourself.'"
MATTHEW 19:19

GOLDEN RULE

EVERY MAJOR RELIGION has its own version of the Golden Rule. Does this fact minimize its importance? Not at all. It shows that God has put it in the hearts of people everywhere to realize this foundational principle of life: If we want to be treated with respect and love, we need to treat others that way first.

The principle seems so simple, but we see it violated every day. All of us long to be accepted—it's the first and foremost desire of every human heart—but we make a sport of behaviors that tear down, rip apart, crush, ignore, and ridicule people around us. Most of us don't actually abuse others. We're too sophisticated for that. Instead, we use gossip, sarcasm, and silence to insert the knife when people don't suspect anything. If we're caught, we say, "Hey, I was just kidding!"

Living by the Golden Rule involves a series of conscious choices to initiate kindness, respect, honor, words of affirmation, and patience to proclaim to someone, "You matter to me!" If we make radical acceptance of others a central value in our lives, amazing things will happen.

Who is the person you know who most lives by the Golden Rule?

What can you do today to take steps to implement it for yourself? Be specific.

LIFE PROMISES

[Jesus said,] "Whoever comes to Me, and hears My sayings and does them, I will show you whom he is like: He is like a man building a house, who dug deep and laid the foundation on the rock. And when the flood arose, the stream beat vehemently against that house, and could not shake it, for it was founded on the rock."

LUKE 6:47-48

Where there is no revelation, the people
     cast off restraint;
    But happy is he who keeps the law.

PROVERBS 29:18

[The Lord said,] "Before I formed you in
     the womb I knew you;
    Before you were born I sanctified
     you."

JEREMIAH 1:5

THE POWER OF VISION

SOME PEOPLE HAVE A CLEAR VISION for their lives, and they gladly subject every aspect of their lives to fulfill their life purpose. Most of us, though, muddle through with only a vague sense of meaning and direction. Some of us dream too much, and some dream too little. Of the two, the latter is worse than the first. If people are moving, they can be steered in a better direction, but if they're stuck, no amount of steering will do any good.

Where does vision originate? Some of us have a personality type that naturally identifies goals and pushes us to achieve them. Others have grown up with parents or other mentors who saw latent potential in us and enflamed the embers of desire to accomplish great things. An imparted vision is just as powerful as one we develop on our own.

But be careful of imparted vision. Many people have powerful goals but are almost completely self-absorbed. Find someone whose purpose in life is to love and serve and build others up—and camp out with that person!

Describe someone you know whose vision is clear, compelling, and centered on others.

Does your sense of purpose need an overhaul? Explain your answer.

LIFE PROMISES

Everyone to whom much is given,
from him much will be required; and
to whom much has been committed,
of him they will ask the more.
LUKE 12:48

Speaking the truth in love, may [we]
grow up in all things into Him who is
the head—Christ.
EPHESIANS 4:15

Mark the blameless man, and observe
     the upright;
  For the future of that man is peace.
PSALM 37:37

WHEN MUCH IS GIVEN

MOST OF US are, by historic and current standards of living, the wealthiest people the world has ever seen. No, we don't have the wealth of Bill Gates or Warren Buffett, but we are fabulously rich.

We can look at our balance sheets in one of two ways: We can compare our net worth with those who have much more and feel inferior, hurt, and a little angry that things haven't worked out as well as we had hoped. Or we can watch the news of drought, famine, floods, and genocidal wars and breathe a deep sigh of relief, realizing we have it made!

There will come a day when we stand before Christ to give an account of all He has entrusted to us. On that day, He won't ask how our balance sheets compared with anyone else's. He'll ask, "What did you do with all I entrusted to you?"

Responsibility prods us to take action, but guilt makes a lousy motivator. A far better push comes from actually investing our resources in the causes God cares about and seeing lives changed.

Where do you see yourself on the scale of "haves" versus "have-nots"?

What would motivate you to invest more of your resources in God's work?

LIFE PROMISES

Whatever is born of God overcomes the world. And this is the victory that has overcome the world—our faith. Who is he who overcomes the world, but he who believes that Jesus is the Son of God?

1 JOHN 5:3-5

You shall remember the LORD your God, for it is He who gives you power to get wealth, that He may establish His covenant which He swore to your fathers, as it is this day.

DEUTERONOMY 8:18

Do not overwork to be rich. . . .
Will you set your eyes on that which
　　　is not?
　　For riches certainly make
　　　themselves wings;
　　They fly away like an eagle toward
　　　heaven.

PROVERBS 23:4-5

OVERCOMING THE WORLD

WE LIVE IN A CULTURE that promises far more than it can deliver. Each and every day, we are barraged by promises of beauty, riches, success, fame, and pleasure. They claim to be able to fill our hearts and give us ultimate happiness, and quite often, we believe their lies. If these promises came to us dressed up as demons in little red suits, we'd recognize them at once and refuse to trust them, but because their lies appear, like Satan himself, as sources of light, we are easily duped.

Why do we need to overcome the world? Because it can overwhelm us and distract us from our relationship with God. These lies steal our attention, erode our faith in God, corrupt our motives, and strain our relationships. Every part of our lives is affected, if not ruined, if we believe the false promises.

Overcoming the world doesn't happen by magic because we say a certain thing or by osmosis because we attend church. In our fight with the world, we overcome when we stay close to Jesus, recognize and reject the lies we hear, and walk in obedience to Him.

What are some of the lies the world tells us? Why do we so readily believe them?

How well are you overcoming the world at this point in your life? What adjustments do you need to make?

LIFE PROMISES

All things were made through Him, and without Him nothing was made that was made.
JOHN 1:3

You formed my inward parts;
   You covered me in my mother's
      womb.
PSALM 139:13

As the elect of God, holy and beloved, put on tender mercies, kindness, humility, meekness, longsuffering; bearing with one another, and forgiving one another, if anyone has a complaint against another; even as Christ forgave you, so you also must do.
COLOSSIANS 3:12-13

CRAFTED BY THE CREATOR

WE'RE ALWAYS CHECKING OURSELVES OUT. We look in the mirror to see how we look, and if we're honest, most of us glance at our reflections in windows throughout the day. We compare our appearance with the models on fashion magazines and celebrities on the red carpet, and we have to face the fact again and again that we don't measure up! As Americans, we spend billions every year to change how we look, and most of us remain disheartened.

We need a new benchmark and new set of values. Almighty God, the One who is infinitely wise, kind, and strong, carefully crafted each of us in the womb. He used the building blocks of DNA, but the uniqueness of our individual appearance was in His hands. However, it was not only our appearance. God crafted our personalities, our intellects, and our talents; and His creative work in each of us prepares us to fulfill the greatest goal life can offer: to be His man or His woman in the circumstances we face every day.

How do you feel about your appearance, intellect, and talents?

How would it change your sense of contentment and passion if you really believed that God crafted you?

LIFE PROMISES

[The Lord] did all this so you would
never say to yourself, "I have achieved
this wealth with my own strength and
energy."
DEUTERONOMY 8:17, NLT

Both riches and honor come from You,
    And You reign over all.
    In Your hand is power and might;
    In Your hand it is to make great
    And to give strength to all.
1 CHRONICLES 29:12

Watch out, or you may be seduced by
        wealth.
    Don't let yourself be bribed into sin.
JOB 36:18, NLT

NEVER ENOUGH

IN ADDICTIONS LIKE ALCOHOLISM, people experience a phenomenon called tolerance. A person's body gets used to the level of alcohol being consumed, so he or she has to drink more to get the same effect. And the process continues as the body adjusts to taking in more and more.

The same phenomenon occurs in the world of money and possessions, but in this case, tolerance is a psychological effect. People believe that the next rung up the ladder will give them the happiness they long for, so they work hard to get there. When they achieve it, they feel great—even euphoric—for a little while. But soon, the feeling wears off, and the next rung comes into view. The pursuit of more always promises ultimate fulfillment, but it always leads to deep disappointment.

The solution to the problem of tolerance in money and possessions isn't to get more and more. It's to kick the habit! We need to step back, take a hard look at the compulsion to acquire, and confess our sin to God. He will forgive us, give us wisdom, and put us on a path of filling our lives with things that really satisfy.

Do you agree or disagree that for many people, the lure to acquire is like an addiction?

What changes do you need to make in your perception of what will really satisfy you?

LIFE PROMISES

Do you not know that those who run
in a race all run, but one receives the
prize? Run in such a way that you may
obtain it.

1 CORINTHIANS 9:24

The steps of a good man are ordered by
      the Lord,
  And He delights in his way.
Though he fall, he shall not be utterly
      cast down;
    For the Lord upholds him with
      His hand.

PSALM 37:23-24

Be renewed in the spirit of your mind,
and . . . put on the new man which
was created according to God, in true
righteousness and holiness.

EPHESIANS 4:23-24

RUN YOUR OWN RACE

WHEN WE CONSTANTLY MEASURE OURSELVES by the successes and failures of others, we run the risk of losing our identity. When we feel insecure, we try to copy those who look successful and we criticize those who mess up. Our goal is to be one up on everybody else. We can't afford to let anybody look better than we do. We live in fear that somebody will find out that we aren't as "put together" as we want them to think, and our relationships suffer. We smile on the outside, but we're worried sick. Some of us have lived this way so long that we don't even realize there's another way to live.

Each of us has our own race to run, and we need to devote our energies to running that race—and only that race—as well as we possibly can. When you realize you're comparing yourself to others, either positively or negatively, remember that you are responsible to run your own race, not someone else's. Running your own race is doing the best you can every chance you get with what you have for a purpose that outlives you.

What are some ways that "comparison kills"?

How would it be helpful for you to focus on running your own race?

LIFE PROMISES

I will praise You, for I am fearfully and
        wonderfully made;
    Marvelous are Your works,
    And that my soul knows very well.
PSALM 139:14

The Spirit of God has made me,
    And the breath of the Almighty
        gives me life.
JOB 33:4

I [Paul] bow my knees to the Father of
our Lord Jesus Christ . . . that He would
grant you . . . to know the love of Christ
which passes knowledge; that you may
be filled with all the fullness of God.
EPHESIANS 3:14, 16, 19

FEARFULLY AND WONDERFULLY MADE

HUMILITY AND CONFIDENCE aren't opposites. They are compatible traits of someone who realizes he or she has been "fearfully and wonderfully made" by God. Everything we are—all our abilities, our intellects, our talents, our skills, and our capabilities—have been hardwired into our DNA by Almighty God or shaped by the experiences He has orchestrated or allowed in our lives. We need to notice how He has crafted us so we maximize our efforts to fit His design.

But take careful note: We are His design, not our own. Yes, we are incredible creatures, but we can't take credit. Even our discipline and desire to excel come from God's work in us. When we realize that God has made us who we are and we appreciate His creative genius, we more eagerly put our lives into His hands.

Pride is ugly and destructive. Actually, most people who appear proud are only covering up their insecurities. The powerful blend of humility and confidence enables us to appreciate our strengths and use them with excellence, but we recognize that we didn't create those abilities. They are gifts from God. And that makes all the difference.

What are the strengths God has hardwired into you or developed in you through experiences?

What difference does it make to realize that God created you with your abilities and that they are gifts from Him to you?

LIFE PROMISES

Better a handful with quietness
    Than both hands full, together
       with toil and grasping for
       the wind.
ECCLESIASTES 4:6

Trust in the LORD with all your heart,
    And lean not on your own
       understanding;
In all your ways acknowledge Him,
    And He shall direct your paths.
PROVERBS 3:5-6

Give to Your servant an understanding
heart to . . . discern between good
and evil.
1 KINGS 3:9

WHEN LESS IS MORE

MANY OF US ARE AFFLICTED with the "go, go, go disease." Somehow, we've developed the core belief that we can't be happy unless we have our lives full of activities. But the disease leaves us feeling exhausted. Our most cherished relationships become shallow and tense, and we become confused because we're trying so hard but feel so empty.

In our light-speed culture, one of the marks of true wisdom is the determination to carve out time and space to reflect, rest, and recharge our emotional batteries. Creating "margin" in our lives doesn't just happen. We have to schedule it, value it, and then protect it from the onslaught of voices that scream, "You've got to do this, too!"

The price we pay for creating these regular times is that we have to say no to some activities, but we need to be honest about the price we've paid for saying yes to too many things. Making margin a priority reduces stress, increases fulfillment, and leads to richer relationships with God and every person in our lives.

What are some of the effects of "go, go, go disease" in your life and in the lives of those you love?

What do you need to do to carve out time and space for yourself?

LIFE PROMISES

Vindicate me, O Lord,
    For I have walked in my integrity.
    I have also trusted in the Lord;
    I shall not slip.
PSALM 26:1

Lying lips are an abomination to
    the Lord,
    But those who deal truthfully
    are His delight.
PROVERBS 12:22

Behold, God will not cast away the
    blameless,
    Nor will He uphold the evildoers.
JOB 8:20

SURE-FOOTED

A CLEAR CONSCIENCE is a glorious thing. When we can go to bed at night without having to relive situations and rethink conversations to make sure we don't get caught in lies, we can enjoy sweet sleep. And when we talk to our spouses and children or look at colleagues at work, we can look them in the eye because we don't have any fear of being caught in fabrications of the truth.

Why do we lie? We may be trying to look good to someone else, we may want to avoid blame for something we've done, or we may have developed a habit of shading the truth. Sometimes truth is glorious, but sometimes it shows our dark side. Either way, we are encouraged to speak truth, live truth, and be an example of truth to others. Trusting God gives us strength to face the sometimes painful facts of our lives. When we've failed, we can embrace God's forgiveness, confess our deception to the person we've lied to, and choose the path of truth again.

How clear is your conscience today?

What would it mean for you to walk in integrity?

Anxiety in the heart of man causes
      depression,
    But a good word makes it glad.

PROVERBS 12:25

Do not worry about your life, what
you will eat or what you will drink; nor
about your body, what you will put on.
Is not life more than food and the body
more than clothing? Look at the birds
of the air, for they neither sow nor reap
nor gather into barns; yet your heavenly
Father feeds them. Are you not of more
value than they?

MATTHEW 6:25-26

Be anxious for nothing, but in everything by prayer and supplication, with
thanksgiving, let your requests be made
known to God.

PHILIPPIANS 4:6

BE TRUE TO YOUR HEART . . . DON'T WORRY!

WHAT DO YOU SPEND MOST OF YOUR TIME thinking about? Many of us never step back and analyze what's running through our minds; we just go with the flow. But when we stop to take notice, we may find that our thoughts are dominated by daydreams of success and worries of failure. A snapshot of our thoughts gives us a picture of the content of our hearts, and what we hold in our hearts serves as the ground, seed, and fertilizer for what grows into our attitudes and actions.

All our thoughts, including our worries and desires to escape, can be filtered through faith, hope, and love. When we're worried, we can refocus our thoughts on the goodness and greatness of God so that we find faith to trust Him for wisdom. When we're bored and want to escape, we can choose to rivet our minds on the hope of God's purpose for us. And when we are thankful, we can let our thoughts roll on in gratitude and love for our Lord.

Analyze your thoughts for the past twenty-four hours. What categories do they fall into?

What can you do today to make better choices about what you think and how you think about them?

LIFE PROMISES

Let no corrupt word proceed out of your mouth, but what is good for necessary edification, that it may impart grace to the hearers. And do not grieve the Holy Spirit of God, by whom you were sealed for the day of redemption.
EPHESIANS 4:29-30

Out of the same mouth proceed blessing and cursing. My brethren, these things ought not to be so.
JAMES 3:10

The lips of the righteous know what is acceptable,
But the mouth of the wicked what is perverse.
PROVERBS 10:32

WORDS YOU CAN BUILD ON

WORDS HAVE THE POWER to heal or destroy, to build up or tear down. Corrupt words of condemnation or name-calling have the force of a sledgehammer to crush people. Gossip and sarcasm are just as destructive, but they are corrosive, taking longer to wear away a person's confidence and ruin a relationship.

We aren't advised to cut back on the harmful words that we say to one another, or to stop saying damaging words. We are commanded to replace these words that tear down with words that build people up.

Every word we utter must meet the standard of God's holiness and love for that person. We should look for good in others and affirm it, and we must notice their successes and celebrate with them. If they have hurt us, we should speak the truth for the purpose of restoration, not condemnation. Our motive changes our language and our demeanor, and perhaps other people's responses.

Our words, though, don't have only a horizontal impact; they also affect the Holy Spirit. The way we speak to one another can grieve the Spirit. Don't miss this. God's emotions are affected by the way we treat one another.

What negative, harmful language do you need to stop using?

Think of three or four common conversations in which you often use crushing or corrosive language, and plan positive statements for each one.

 ## LIFE PROMISES

Blessed are the meek,
> For they shall inherit the earth.

MATTHEW 5:5

My flesh and my heart fail;
> But God is the strength of my heart
> and my portion forever.

PSALM 73:26

God is able to make all grace abound
toward you, that you, always having all
sufficiency in all things, may have an
abundance for every good work.

2 CORINTHIANS 9:8

MEEK AIN'T WEAK

THE WORD *MEEK* has a bad reputation. Most people hear it and think of someone cowering in timidity, but that's not what the word means. It actually means "power under control," like the strength and beauty of a champion racehorse under the direction of an expert jockey.

Meekness doesn't come naturally. Often, we see the opposite extreme of angry defiance or wilting fear. Meekness isn't a blend of those two traits; it's altogether different. God has given all of us a set of abilities and character qualities. Meekness acknowledges that all our abilities and qualities are gifts from the hand of God, but we also recognize that we distort God's original intentions when we pursue selfish aims.

Like the horse responding to the jockey's directions, we move in concert with God's instruction. And like the horse, we may sometimes need a little stronger motivation! When we allow God's Spirit to direct us, a world of possibilities opens up to us. That's what it means to inherit the earth.

How would you define meekness?

What would your life look like if your strengths were under God's guidance?

LIFE PROMISES

I am the LORD, I do not change.
MALACHI 3:6

Like a cloak You will fold them up,
    And they will be changed.
    But You are the same,
    And Your years will not fail.
HEBREWS 1:12

I will wait for You, O You his Strength;
    For God is my defense.
PSALM 59:9

SOME MORE THAN OTHERS

CHANGE IS DIFFICULT. Studies show that people fear change almost as much as speaking in public. In fact, the fear of change is the most common fear we experience. When our world is shaken, we lose our bearings, we feel insecure, and we grasp for anything that can bring us certainty. Though *our* world may be shaken, *God*'s world remains steady and solid. Change never threatens God because He knows what is going to happen before it happens, and He sees the end with crystal clarity when we see our future through a mist.

A common reaction to change is worry. We believe that if we think about our problem enough, we can figure it out. Sometimes that's true, but often, our copious reflections lead only to more worry, more confusion, and genuine despair. When we start to worry, we can remember that God knows everything about every aspect of the change we're experiencing. His infinite knowledge and His genuine compassion can relieve our worries and give us confidence in His future for us, no matter what.

How do you normally respond to change?

When we experience change, how is it helpful to remember that God is omniscient?

LIFE PROMISES

Blessed are the merciful,
For they shall obtain mercy.
MATTHEW 5:7

Love your enemies, do good, and lend,
hoping for nothing in return; and your
reward will be great, and you will be
sons of the Most High. For He is kind to
the unthankful and evil.
LUKE 6:35

Sin shall not have dominion over you,
for you are not under law but under
grace.
ROMANS 6:14

A LITTLE KINDNESS

IF YOU WANT TO BE ON THE RECEIVING END of kindness, you have to show kindness to others first. It's the law of sowing and reaping. Mercy is responding compassionately to someone's hurt, going the extra mile to help people in need, and being willing to listen when someone wants to talk.

Those who delight in justice want to see the guilty punished, wrongs righted, and boxes checked off so that they can move on to more pleasant things in life. But hurting people are all around us, and they'll always be here. Some are obvious, some are hidden, and some live in the same house as we do.

If our instant response to others in need is, "Well, they get what they deserve," then we haven't realized that, by God's grace, we *don't* get what we really deserve. If we have difficulty showing mercy, then we first need to go to the Cross to realize the wealth of God's grace, mercy, kindness, and forgiveness given to us. With this realization fresh on our hearts, we'll be quicker to extend mercy to others in need around us.

Describe a time when someone extended mercy to you. How did it affect you?

How would it affect your most difficult relationship if you were merciful to that person?

LIFE PROMISES

Those who wait on the LORD
    Shall renew their strength;
    They shall mount up with wings
        like eagles,
    They shall run and not be weary,
    They shall walk and not faint.
ISAIAH 40:31

Truly my soul silently waits for God;
    From Him comes my salvation.
PSALM 62:1

The LORD will wait, that He may be
        gracious to you;
    And therefore He will be exalted,
        that He may have mercy on you.
    For the LORD is a God of justice;
    Blessed are all those who wait
        for Him.
ISAIAH 30:18

THE SECRET
OF PERSEVERANCE

WAITING IS SUCH A DRAG. Most of us hate waiting with
a passion! When we get in any line (at a red light, at the
grocery-store checkout, at a ticket window, or anywhere
else), we first scan the available lines to see which one
might move fastest, and after we make our choice, we
watch the people who got in the other lines when we
got in ours. If any of them move faster, we boil!

Waiting is an essential part of God's plan for our
lives, but it's not just killing time. When we "wait on the
LORD," our focus is on Him, His goals, and His path for
us. We wait expectantly, not impatiently, because we are
increasingly convinced that God is up to something—
something good—that we haven't experienced before.

The secret of perseverance isn't to grit our teeth as
time passes. The secret is to focus. We wait expectantly,
trusting that a good, wise, all-knowing God will accomplish His gracious purposes in His good time. We trust
that while we wait He's preparing the situation, other
people, or us for something special.

Describe a time when you had to wait on God.

*What difference did it make (or will it make next time)
for you to focus your heart on God's character and trust
His purposes while waiting?*

 ## LIFE PROMISES

He has made everything beautiful in its time. Also He has put eternity in their hearts, except that no one can find out the work that God does from beginning to end.

ECCLESIASTES 3:11

I will instruct you and teach you in the
way you should go;
I will guide you with My eye.

PSALM 32:8

To everything there is a season,
A time for every purpose under
heaven.

ECCLESIASTES 3:1

ETERNITY IN THEIR HEARTS

IN EVERY AGE, culture, religion, and nation, people have an innate awareness that life transcends what they can see, taste, feel, and smell. All of them know that a supernatural world exists, though they may pursue it in different ways. People may try to define the supernatural world or categorize it into "steps" or "paths" or "gods" or "laws," but their meager attempts to put labels on God fall far short. Even we Christians, who have the truth of the Scriptures to tell us about God, recognize that He is far greater than we can conceive.

Creation shouts that God exists, and history declares that He became a man and died for our sins two millennia ago. About these things, we can be certain. But in this life, we often can't see the hand of God working in individual lives—especially our own! His ways are mysterious and sometimes bewildering.

Great art often combines certainty and mystery to intrigue us. That's part of what makes it beautiful. In the same way, God blends those traits in our lives and in our world to make "everything beautiful in its time."

Do you feel more comfortable with certainty or with mystery?

What are some reasons you need the other trait in your life and in your walk with God?

LIFE PROMISES

I take pleasure in infirmities, in reproaches, in needs, in persecutions, in distresses, for Christ's sake. For when I am weak, then I am strong.
2 CORINTHIANS 12:10

Fear not, for I am with you;
Be not dismayed, for I am your God.
I will strengthen you,
Yes, I will help you,
I will uphold you with My righteous
right hand.
ISAIAH 41:10

In the day when I cried out, You
answered me,
And made me bold with strength
in my soul.
PSALM 138:3

STRENGTH IN WEAKNESS

MANY YEARS AGO, a man was arrested in the Soviet Union. After a sham trial, he was sentenced to twenty years of hard labor in the Siberian gulag. Seven days a week, fourteen hours a day, he worked in fierce cold in winter and swarms of ravenous insects in summer. Some men died from exhaustion, and most of the survivors became bitter and hardened. This man, though, found Christ, and his days of labor took on new meaning. He learned to thank God for the meager food ration the prisoners were given, and he learned to experience joy in that desolate place.

Suffering is a given for us. We naturally try to construct our lives to avoid it if at all possible, but sooner or later, suffering weasels its way into our experience. At that moment, we either embrace it as a tutor to teach us the deepest, richest lessons of life, or we despise suffering and our hearts grow hard and cold.

Weakness isn't fun and isn't pretty, but admitting our weaknesses to God is the first step in trusting Him and experiencing His great strength.

How do you normally respond to suffering?

How would it help to believe God can turn suffering into something good in your life?

LIFE PROMISES

As you therefore have received Christ Jesus the Lord, so walk in Him, rooted and built up in Him and established in the faith, as you have been taught, abounding in it with thanksgiving.
COLOSSIANS 2:6-7

Let us therefore come boldly to the throne of grace, that we may obtain mercy and find grace to help in time of need.
HEBREWS 4:16

Behold, I long for Your precepts;
    Revive me in Your righteousness.
PSALM 119:40

WHEN LIFE DOESN'T SEEM FAIR

YOU WORKED HARD in the company for years, but someone else got the promotion. You invested your money in funds your broker recommended, but they plunged to the bottom of the Morningstar ratings. You did your best to be a good parent, but your kids turned out to be no better than the children whose parents didn't seem to care about them.

Many times, unbelievers do just as well in life as believers. What's that about? If we take out our measuring stick too often, we can become angry because we think we deserve more than we're getting from God.

Jesus spent a lot of His time explaining the grace of God to people. Grace is a foreign concept to most of us. We operate by standards, rewards, and punishments, so grace just doesn't fit. When we see God's grace operate in the lives of people who we feel don't deserve it, we have a choice: Either we can complain and feel sorry for ourselves, or we can be thankful that the God of such goodness is the One we love and serve. Comparison kills because it always leaves us wanting more, but thankfulness brings life.

In your opinion, who are some people who are getting more than they deserve?

How does comparison kill, and how does thankfulness give life?

LIFE PROMISES

[Jesus said,] "I say to you that for every idle word men may speak, they will give account of it in the day of judgment. For by your words you will be justified, and by your words you will be condemned."
MATTHEW 12:36-37

The mouth of the righteous speaks
        wisdom,
    And his tongue talks of justice.
PSALM 37:30

A man's stomach shall be satisfied from
        the fruit of his mouth;
    From the produce of his lips he shall
        be filled.
PROVERBS 18:20

WEIGH YOUR WORDS

OUR WORDS HAVE THE POWER to heal or to destroy. Our choices in using them make a difference in people's lives, and God will judge those choices when we stand before Him to give an account of our lives. On that day, we can't say, "Oh, that's not what I meant," or "She didn't understand," or "I was just joking."

We can understand that really important statements will receive God's attention: defending a friend with courage, lovingly affirming a spouse at a critical moment of self-doubt, confronting the Little League coach for not playing a son enough, or lying to a parent. But even our most off-the-cuff remarks undergo God's scrutiny because they, too, have the power to heal or to destroy. A spontaneous word of praise can make someone's day, or a careless whisper of gossip can ruin a reputation.

The gravity of Jesus' statement makes us stop short and ask, "Whoa, this must be pretty important. What do I say that needs more attention?" What, indeed.

How have you seen seemingly insignificant remarks heal or destroy someone?

How could you speak more words of encouragement and avoid criticisms and condemnation—even in the most casual conversations?

 **LIFE PROMISES**

Blessed be the God and Father of our
Lord Jesus Christ, the Father of mercies
and God of all comfort, who comforts
us in all our tribulation, that we may be
able to comfort those who are in any
trouble, with the comfort with which
we ourselves are comforted by God.
2 CORINTHIANS 1:3-4

Yea, though I walk through the valley
    of the shadow of death,
  I will fear no evil;
  For You are with me;
  Your rod and Your staff, they
    comfort me.
PSALM 23:4

[Jesus said,] "These things I have
spoken to you, that in Me you may
have peace. In the world you will
have tribulation; but be of good
cheer, I have overcome the world."
JOHN 16:33

BRINGING COMFORT

NOBODY LIKES PAIN. We naturally wonder, *Where is God when it hurts?* and *Why is this happening?* The Scriptures tell us that suffering may occur from a variety of causes, including natural disasters, the consequences of our own sins, and the effects of others' sins against us. Whatever the cause, and whether we ever figure it out, our response can include two things: turning to God for comfort and then comforting others who are in pain.

God never promised a pain-free life. Instead, God promises that our pain will never be in vain. No matter what we experience and whether we ever learn the reason or not, God is willing to enter into our pain with us, to give us a sense of His presence, and to provide genuine comfort for us. The process may be short or long, but if we cling to God, we'll experience His mercy and comfort. Then, and only then, will we be able to comfort others who feel just as much despair, emptiness, and heartache as we felt in the midst of our pain.

Describe a time when you were hurting. What questions did you ask? What brought real comfort?

Who are some people around you today who need to be comforted? What will you do?

LIFE PROMISES

I will give you the treasures of darkness
    And hidden riches of secret places,
    That you may know that I, the LORD,
    Who call you by your name,
    Am the God of Israel.
ISAIAH 45:3

Yes, the Almighty will be your gold
    And your precious silver.
JOB 22:25

I [Paul] want you to know what a
great conflict I have for you . . . and
for as many as have not seen my face
in the flesh, that their hearts may be
encouraged, being knit together in
love, and attaining to all riches of the
full assurance of understanding, to
the knowledge of the mystery of God,
both of the Father and of Christ, in
whom are hidden all the treasures of
wisdom and knowledge.
COLOSSIANS 2:1-3

TREASURES FROM THE DARK

THE THOUGHT OF FINDING A TREASURE has thrilled people from the beginning of time. Ancient cultures told myths about it, and today, millions watch as lottery numbers are posted each day. Some treasures require years of search and sacrifice.

In the book of Isaiah, a completely different kind of treasure is described. In the most difficult and most excruciating moments of our lives, God wants us to find a treasure. When times are good, we roll along with only a superficial pursuit of God, but in our pain, we cry out to Him from the deepest recesses of our souls. We desperately need to know Him, His heart, and His purpose for us right then. In that cry for help, God reveals Himself to us so that we grasp more of His character. We may not know why something happened, but that matters less if we know we can trust the One who holds all things in His hands. That's true treasure.

We never manufacture times of darkness so that we can find this treasure, but when these times occur, we can have confidence that God will meet us there.

What are some times of darkness you've experienced?

In what ways is knowing God more deeply and intimately true treasure to you?

LIFE PROMISES

Oh, give thanks to the Lord, for He
is good!
For His mercy endures forever.
1 CHRONICLES 16:34

Continue earnestly in prayer, being
vigilant in it with thanksgiving.
COLOSSIANS 4:2

Enter into His gates with thanksgiving,
And into His courts with praise.
Be thankful to Him, and bless
His name.
PSALM 100:4

REALLY THANKFUL

IT'S A DELIGHT to be around thankful people. They fill up a room with their optimism, thoughtfulness, and peace. However, each of us knows people who seldom have anything positive to say. Even when things go well, their cynicism sours people around them.

What makes people thankful? They are known for two connected actions: remembering God's past blessings and realizing that God still gives them wonderful gifts. They look forward to the future, trusting that the One who has abundantly provided will provide yet again. Don't assume that thankful people are blind to the often painful realities in life. In fact, they can be more honest about hurts and disappointments because they don't need to hide from those things. But their hope focuses their attention away from their hurts and disappointments and onto God's character. They are convinced that sooner or later He will give them the wisdom, strength, direction, and blessing they need. Looking back at God's past faithfulness gives them confidence in Him for the future.

Who is the best example in your life of someone who is an honest and thankful person?

As you look back as well as forward, what needs to happen for you to take steps to become more thankful?

LIFE PROMISES

[Jesus said,] "I say to you, love your
enemies, bless those who curse you, do
good to those who hate you, and pray
for those who spitefully use you and
persecute you."
MATTHEW 5:44

One man of you shall chase a thousand,
for the LORD your God is He who fights
for you, as He promised you.
JOSHUA 23:10

The LORD is for me among those who
      help me;
    Therefore I shall see my desire on
      those who hate me.
PSALM 118:7

CAN YOU LOVE
YOUR ENEMIES?

IT MAKES PERFECT SENSE to love people who love us and hate those who hate us. That's just the way the world works!

But it's not the way the Kingdom works. Jesus wants us to go completely against our basic human natures and love the people who annoy or antagonize us, do kind things for the people who actively try to hurt us, and ask God's blessing for those who curse us and do everything in their power to cause us pain.

It doesn't make sense—until we realize that's exactly the way God has treated us. We had nothing to offer Him except our arrogance, rebellion, and apathy. We were so preoccupied with our own selfish desires that we didn't think much about other people or God. But through it all, God loved us when we deserved only punishment.

In any relationship, and especially any strained relationship, we have a choice. If we choose selfishness, we're on our own, but if we make the hard decision to make our lives a display case of His grace, He has promised to lead us, fill us, and use us to change lives.

In what ways is loving the unlovely like God?

What steps can you take today to be a display case of God's grace?

LIFE PROMISES

Who may ascend into the hill of the
       LORD?
    Or who may stand in His holy place?
He who has clean hands and a
       pure heart,
    Who has not lifted up his soul
       to an idol,
    Nor sworn deceitfully.
PSALM 24:3-4

We . . . will not boast beyond measure,
but within the limits of the sphere
which God appointed us— a sphere
which especially includes you.
2 CORINTHIANS 10:13

If anyone cleanses himself . . . he will be
a vessel for honor, sanctified and useful
for the Master, prepared for every good
work. Flee also youthful lusts; but
pursue righteousness, faith, love, peace
with those who call on the Lord out of a
pure heart.
2 TIMOTHY 2:21-22

KING OF THE MOUNTAIN

IN THE BUSINESS WORLD, many people get to the top by climbing over others on the way. They want to be "king of the hill," and nothing or nobody is going to stop them. But in the spiritual world, the goal isn't to stand in power in front of shareholders; it's to stand in humility and inner strength before the Lord.

In the awkward time between his anointing and his coronation as king, David had many opportunities to take shortcuts and compromise his integrity. But each time, David refused to rush to success. He trusted God to accomplish His purposes in His timing. Through times of being misunderstood, attacked, and betrayed, David had "clean hands and a pure heart." He trusted God even in the darkest days, and he kept telling the truth.

One of the most significant features of David's life was the loyalty of his men. In him they saw a man they could trust, a man who spoke the unvarnished truth and followed God with his whole heart.

What are some temptations to take shortcuts to gain promotions at work?

What does it take for someone to act like David did and keep "clean hands and a pure heart"?

LIFE PROMISES

Trust in the LORD with all your heart,
  And lean not on your own
    understanding.

PROVERBS 3:5

Give all your worries and cares to God,
for he cares about you.

1 PETER 5:7, NLT

The LORD shall preserve your going out
    and your coming in
  From this time forth, and even
    forevermore.

PSALM 121:8

GOOD ADVICE

OUR IMMEDIATE AND NATURAL INSTINCT is to trust what we can see, touch, and feel and to rely on our ability to figure out solutions to any problem. When the chips are down, we "lean" on our ability to analyze situations and figure out what to do next.

In fact, many of us become obsessed with figuring out what to do when times are tough. It is called "worry." We can't concentrate on the job in front of us because we're still thinking about the problem, situation, or comment that absorbs our minds. We can't sleep because we go over our fears and our plans again and again. We create scenarios and weigh options. We try to imagine others' responses, and our fears compound.

Our instinct, though, is flawed and limited. Another source of wisdom is far superior to our ability to figure things out. We are connected with the God of the universe, the One who knows all, sees all, and is powerfully able to accomplish anything He desires. The more we grasp this fundamental fact of the Christian faith, the more we will learn to overcome our instincts and trust in an unseen but all-seeing God.

In your experience, what are some differences between leaning on your own understanding and trusting in God?

What are some situations you face now in which you need to trust more in God? What will you trust Him to do?

Oh, give thanks to the Lord!
    Call upon His name;
    Make known His deeds among
        the peoples!
1 CHRONICLES 16:8

Every creature of God is good, and
nothing is to be refused if it is received
with thanksgiving.
1 TIMOTHY 4:4

Oh, give thanks to the Lord, for He
        is good!
    For His mercy endures forever.
PSALM 136:1

AN ATTITUDE OF GRATITUDE

COMPARISON KILLS A THANKFUL HEART. Far too often, we look around at what others have, and gradually (or not so gradually), discontent takes over. Comparison convinces us that whatever we have isn't enough. Raises, bonuses, and windfalls of any kind satisfy only for a moment, and we quickly revert back to demanding more and more. Chasing the dream sounds exciting, but it can lead to a hardened heart.

Instead, Paul reminds the believers in Corinth that God had already poured out His riches of grace on them. They had gone from condemned prisoners to beloved children of the King! They had been spiritual paupers, and now they were rich beyond measure in God's blessings. They had been lost and impotent, wandering through life without hope, but now they "reigned as kings"!

Each of us looks in a mirror every day, either the mirror of earthly success and approval, which tells us we never have enough, or the mirror of God's grace and truth, which says we're already rich. Which one do you believe?

How are you affected (attitude, desires, demands, actions) by comparison?

How would it change your life if you looked more often in the mirror of God's grace and truth, which says you're already rich?

See 1 Corinthians 4:8.

LIFE PROMISES

My brethren, count it all joy when you
fall into various trials, knowing that the
testing of your faith produces patience.
JAMES 1:2-3

Call upon Me in the day of trouble;
    I will deliver you, and you shall
        glorify Me.
PSALM 50:15

Our light affliction, which is but for a
moment, is working for us a far more
exceeding and eternal weight of glory.
2 CORINTHIANS 4:17

EYES ON THE OUTCOME

MANY CHRISTIANS simply don't believe that suffering will produce what God says it will, and those who do believe often feel frustrated and defeated because they don't see the result He promised. *Count it all joy? Oh, come on!*

To see trials produce results in our lives, we need to undergo a radical reorientation. But in the Kingdom of God, He treasures our faith in Him through thick and thin, and He knows faith is built most effectively in times of difficulty. For that reason, God, our loving and attentive Father, allows or orchestrates problems in our lives so that we learn to trust Him.

Author and speaker Elisabeth Elliot notes that suffering takes all kinds of forms. Her broad definition is, "Not having what you want, or having what you don't want." Every obstacle, every annoyance, and every genuine heartache in our lives is part of God's curriculum to produce persistent, tenacious, rich, deep trust in Him. Patience isn't killing time until we experience more personal peace and affluence. It's riveting our affections on God and His purposes every moment of every day.

What are some ways the pursuit of "personal peace and affluence" erode patient and persistent faith in God?

How would it help you to realize that every difficulty in your life is part of God's curriculum to teach you faith and patience?

Whoever guards his mouth and tongue
    Keeps his soul from troubles.
PROVERBS 21:23

May the Lord cut off all flattering lips,
    And the tongue that speaks proud
        things.
PSALM 12:3

Set a guard, O Lord, over my mouth;
    Keep watch over the door of my lips.
PSALM 141:3

WELL, SHUT MY MOUTH!

WE CAN KEEP OUR SOULS from trouble—the trouble that comes from saying dumb things—only if we actively guard our mouths. Here are some common-sense suggestions that can change your life:

> Every morning, ask God for wisdom about your words.

> Before any significant conversation, take a minute to define your goals. Also, identify any topics or issues to avoid or treat diplomatically.

> Watch out for any temptation to use sarcasm to get a laugh. (Stopping that habit may severely limit the number of words some of us use!)

> In conversations, be aware that words can kill or cure. If you feel emotions rising, take a deep breath and don't let your words fly!

> From time to time, give yourself a progress report on how well you're guarding your mouth.

For all of us, learning a new skill takes time and effort. And for some of us, the learning curve for guarding our words is really steep. Still, peace of mind and the joy of good relationships are worth the effort.

In what specific kinds of situations does your mouth get you in trouble?

What steps will you take today to guard your mouth?

LIFE PROMISES

Be imitators of God as dear children.
And walk in love, as Christ also has
loved us and given Himself for us, an
offering and a sacrifice to God for a
sweet-smelling aroma.
EPHESIANS 5:1-2

Concerning brotherly love you have no
need that I should write to you, for you
yourselves are taught by God to love
one another.
1 THESSALONIANS 4:9

We love each other because he loved
us first.
1 JOHN 4:19, NLT

GIVE YOURSELF AWAY

IN A SENSE, all of us give ourselves away to the people around us every day, but what do we give? God wants us to give ourselves to others in the same way Jesus gave Himself to us: unreservedly—with kindness, boldness, and amazing love—taking great risks of being misunderstood and rejected.

When we think about those traits and the impact they have on others, it's easy to envision a huge, fragrant, beautiful bouquet of flowers filling the room with their wonderful scent. All our senses are drawn to the bouquet, and we delight in it, not rushing along to check off the next thing on our to-do lists. God wants each of us to have that kind of impact on people around us because of the sweetness and love we show them.

The source of our love for others is our experience of the deep, rich, transforming love of God. We can look at it from another angle too: If we don't demonstrate much love for people around us, perhaps we need to experience more of God's love to fill our tanks so they overflow in love for those around us.

What, do you think, do you smell like to others?

What do you need to do to fill your tank with God's love for you?

Evil men do not understand justice,
    But those who seek the Lord
        understand all.
PROVERBS 28:5

Men will say,
    "Surely there is a reward for the
        righteous;
    Surely He is God who judges in
        the earth."
PSALM 58:11

Keep justice, and do righteousness,
For My salvation is about to come,
And My righteousness to be revealed.
ISAIAH 56:1

SHIFTING LIFE'S PARADIGM

IN THE HEART OF EACH OF US, we have an innate sense of justice. At the core of our souls, our conscience tells us the difference between right and wrong. But when someone has pursued selfish ends long enough and hard enough, that sense of justice is clouded. Self-absorbed people experience a lot of disappointment and anger, and they often have a hair trigger when it comes to accusing God or anyone else who doesn't meet their demands.

We experience wonderful moments when life is good, and at other times, we suffer through deep valleys of heartache. Much of the time, we march along life's trails with friends and family, enjoying everyday blessings and overcoming obstacles. On this journey, we develop wisdom, as well as the ability to see beneath the surface and grasp the fact that God knows exactly what He's doing, even when we don't.

Wise people realize that in this life some things aren't fair, and they can live with that fact because they know that in the next life, a righteous Judge will make all things right.

What are some things that cause people to say, "Life's not fair"?

What's the connection between trusting God and acquiring wisdom?

LIFE PROMISES

In all your ways acknowledge Him,
And He shall direct your paths.
PROVERBS 3:6

The righteous will hold to his way,
And he who has clean hands will
be stronger and stronger.
JOB 17:9

We . . . do not cease to pray for you, and
to ask that you may be filled with the
knowledge of His will in all wisdom and
spiritual understanding; that you may
walk worthy of the Lord, fully pleasing
Him, being fruitful in every good
work and increasing in the knowledge
of God.
COLOSSIANS 1:9-10

BURNING BRIGHT, NOT BURNING OUT

JESUS NEVER LET POPULARITY go to His head, and He didn't let opposition get Him off track. Throughout His ministry, He kept His eyes fixed on the purpose the Father had given Him. Early in His ministry, He was immensely popular; however, nothing, not even the greatest successes and popularity, could keep Jesus from doing what He came to do: tell everyone everywhere the Good News.

Both failure and success can drive us to exhaustion. Failure fills us with fear and shame, and we dedicate ourselves to avoid failure at all costs. But success can be intoxicating. The adrenaline rush propels us to do more, be more, and please people more, but before long, our emotional tank runs dry. The only way we can burn bright without burning out is to rivet our hearts on God's purpose and stay true to it through the ups of success and popularity and the downs of failure and despair. Either way, we should focus on God's purpose, and say no to anything that gets in the way.

How can fear of failure or the intoxication of success take our eyes off God's purpose for our lives?

Do you need to make a midcourse correction at this point?

LIFE PROMISES

Praise the LORD,
>   for he has shown me the wonders
>   of his unfailing love.

PSALM 31:21, NLT

The LORD is my strength and song,
>   And He has become my salvation;
>   He is my God, and I will praise Him;
>   My father's God, and I will exalt Him.

EXODUS 15:2

By Him let us continually offer the
sacrifice of praise to God, that is, the
fruit of our lips, giving thanks to His
name.

HEBREWS 13:15

TRUE PRAISE

WHAT DO YOU PRAISE? Most of us praise our favorite sports team, a great restaurant, a great band, successful companies, or the courage of a hero we admire. When we praise these things, what do we do? We shine a light on their most positive attributes, calling attention to them so that others will think highly of these things too.

How do we feel when we praise something or someone? We are emotionally engaged, excited about others' knowing what we know and feeling what we feel. But we utter genuine praise only when our hearts are connected to the thing we're praising. Otherwise, it's just empty chatter.

On one side of the capstone of the Washington Monument, 555 feet high, a plaque reads "*Laus Deo*," meaning "praise to God." The builders wanted to be sure that God received the credit for their work and their nation, so they engraved these Latin words permanently at the top. You and I have the same opportunity every day to give God credit for all He has given us, including our ability to work and to care for and help others.

What or whom do you praise most often? Does God seem as wonderful as that thing or person ? Why or why not?

What are some ways praise can become more central to your daily life?

LIFE PROMISES

Fulfill my joy by being like-minded, having the same love, being of one accord, of one mind. Let nothing be done through selfish ambition or conceit, but in lowliness of mind let each esteem others better than himself. Let each of you look out not only for his own interests, but also for the interests of others.
PHILIPPIANS 2:2-4

Whoever desires to save his life will lose it, but whoever loses his life for My sake will find it.
MATTHEW 16:25

Let no one seek his own, but each one the other's well-being.
1 CORINTHIANS 10:24

LIFE'S PARADOX

THE PARADOX OF LIFE is that by giving, we receive; by sacrificing, we gain; and by putting others first, we feel fulfilled. Some people get it. Newborn babies certainly don't have much success or many skills to offer, but they give their mothers and fathers tremendous joy as they care for them. Employers who celebrate their people's successes more than their own reap the joy of their employees' smiles and their greater productivity, the natural product of feeling affirmed.

We experience this paradox, however, only when we start at the right point: "lowliness of mind." Thinking properly about ourselves is the first step. Instead of selfish ambition to achieve status, we feel secure in God's love. Instead of conceit that we're better than others, we value others highly. Some people confuse humility with shame, but humility doesn't mean we despise ourselves and demean our abilities. Instead, it means that we see our abilities as gifts from God to be used to build others up and accomplish His purposes. As we see all we have and all we are as gifts from God, we can stop promoting or defending ourselves, and we can focus our attention on others around us.

Why, do you think, are most people (and even many Christians) so self-focused?

What would it take for you to live this paradox? How would it impact your relationships?

LIFE PROMISES

Brethren, I do not count myself to have apprehended; but one thing I do, forgetting those things which are behind and reaching forward to those things which are ahead, I press toward the goal for the prize of the upward call of God in Christ Jesus.

PHILIPPIANS 3:12-14

The Lord will perfect that which
        concerns me;
    Your mercy, O Lord, endures
        forever;
    Do not forsake the works of
        Your hands.

PSALM 138:8

We know that all things work together for good to those who love God, to those who are the called according to His purpose.

ROMANS 8:28

EXCESS BAGGAGE

WHEN OLYMPIC MARATHON RUNNERS get ready for a race, they give plenty of attention to their gear. Shorts and shirts are made of the thinnest, lightest material. Most runners don't wear socks, and if they do, the socks are very lightweight. Their shoes, the heaviest item in their wardrobes, have gone through technological transformations so they are as light as can be. Nothing is going to slow down these runners.

The writer of Hebrews compared the Christian life to a long-distance race, and he told us to get rid of excess baggage and sin in our lives. Many of us carry around *baggage* of neglected areas that have become bloated or weak, such as how much money we spend, a lack of exercise, or too little time with our families. Our *sins* are areas of disobedience that weigh us down with guilt and fog our vision of God's purpose in our lives.

When we look to Jesus and are free from the weight of baggage and sin, we can run toward Him and His purpose for our lives even faster.

What are some things that are slowing you down in your race of faith?

What are you going to do today about those things?

See Hebrews 12:1-2.

SCRIPTURE INDEX

ABOUT THE AUTHOR

ZIG ZIGLAR is a motivational teacher and trainer who has traveled the world over, delivering his messages of humor, hope, and encouragement. As a talented author and speaker, he has international appeal that transcends every color, culture, and career. Recognized by his peers as the quintessential motivational genius of our times, Zig Ziglar has a unique delivery style and powerful messages that have earned him many honors. Today he is considered one of the most versatile authorities on the science of human potential. Ten of his twenty-eight books have been on bestseller lists, and his titles have been translated into more than thirty-eight languages and dialects. He is a committed family man, a dedicated patriot, and an active church member. Zig lives in Plano, Texas, with his wife, Jean.

Also available from
Tyndale House Publishers

GET
DAILY ENCOURAGEMENT, WISDOM,
AND INSIGHT FROM CLASSIC BOOKS, AUTHORS,
AND SPEAKERS.